D0577324

THE TIMES

Her Majesty Queen Elizabeth the

QUEEN MOTHER

THE TIMES

Her Majesty Queen Elizabeth the

QUEEN MOTHER

—— Alan Hamilton ——

A UNIQUE CELEBRATION OF HER LIFE

TED SMART

This edition produced for
The Book People
Hall Wood Avenue
Haydock
St Helen's WA11 9UL

First published in 1999
by Times Books
HarperCollins*Publishers*
77-85 Fulham Palace Road
London W6 8JB

Copyright © Times Newspapers Ltd 1999

All rights reserved. No part of this book may be reproduced, stored in a
retrieval system, or transmitted in any form or by any means electronic,
mechanical, photocopying, recording or otherwise without the prior
written permission of the publisher and copyright owner.

Printed and bound in Great Britain by the Bath Press Ltd

Editorial Direction: Juliette Bright.
Picture Editor: Suzanne Hodgart.
Picture Researcher: Alison Rogers.
Proofreader: Mark Denby.

Designed by Liz Brown

British Cataloguing in Publication Data
A catalogue record for this book is available from the British Library
ISBN   0 583 34582 4

**The publishers gratefully acknowledge the assistance of the
managers and staff of the News International Imaging, Commercial
Printing, and Syndication departments, the Electronic Picture
Library, The Times Reference and Picture Libraries, and Archive
for their help in the making of this book.**

CONTENTS

INTRODUCTION

We marvel at little in these clever times, yet great lives still have the power to intrigue us. We consider ourselves a society of equals far more than we ever did before, yet we are still fascinated by the deeds of the grand, the famous and the shapers of history. Queen Elizabeth the Queen Mother is such a figure, and the facets of her appeal are many.

Her remarkable life encompasses the 20th century with a neat and convenient precision. Her birth occurred in the middle distance of history, when Queen Victoria was in her last year of life. She has witnessed more turbulence and change in the world than during most other lifetimes. She was born before the Wright Brothers made the first heavier-than-air flight and has seen men land on the moon, photograph Jupiter and circumnavigate the globe in a tricycle with wings. In that span she has witnessed two world wars, the beginning and end of the communist empire and the complete dissolution of British imperial power. She was born to the telegram and lives to see the Internet.

She has not been a mere spectator to history; she has played a significant part in it. She brought fresh blood to the tired Hanoverian genes of the British throne, and proved her worth in large measure when fate cast her in the role of Queen Consort to a nation at war and in danger of losing.

As Queen Consort and latterly as Queen Mother she displays the virtues of stamina, wisdom and a sense of both duty and vocation. Throughout her long life she has been ambitious towards position, enjoyment and fulfilment, all of which she has unquestionably achieved.

Her talent has been to be the grandest lady in the land without ever appearing so; her greatest contribution to the British throne, and to the world at large, has been her personality. On the occasion of her 80th birthday, *The Times* observed: "Making royalty

human is what she has achieved. Who else could plant the third- or fourth-thousandth tree of a lifetime of planting trees and still leave on the Lady Mayoress the impression of really being pleased to meet her? What is more, of whom else would that impression be true?"

As a child, she displayed a self-assurance that bordered on precocity. In old age, she retains an unquenchable appetite for meeting people, and an ability to raise their spirits by convincing them that they are the object of her undivided interest. No Hollywood queen was ever quite so good with her public.

Elizabeth may be regarded as our last Eminent Victorian, upholding the virtues and values of that age throughout her life – a belief in God, duty, the sanctity of marriage and hard work. But as the 20th century progressed, those very values seemed ever more at odds with a world of shifting perceptions.

From the moment that her elder daughter succeeded in 1952, Elizabeth has remained a powerful influence on Royal Family affairs, a queen behind the throne. Historians may well argue that without her potent voice in family councils the monarchy might well have been more willing to adapt to the late 20th century rather than always having to be pushed. It was inevitable that she should be seen as the last surviving link with stable and immutable monarchy – her own contribution to its stability in the days of George VI was immense – but the days of Victoria are a century gone and the world is a different place.

The balance of history will nonetheless be on her side. Her daughter commands respect and admiration for a dutiful, if sometimes trying, reign. What Elizabeth has commanded, above all, is affection. For all her high principles, she has brought monarchy to the people and made them believe it had worth. She has always seemed real.

The greater her age, the more she becomes an inspiration to the elderly, maintaining her customary vigour through two hip replacements. It is a common observation that the achievement of longevity is easy for one excused a life of manual labour or money worries, but there are few who begrudge her generous parliamentary annuity or her separate court at Clarence House. Even the most astringent critics of monarchical flummery and expense succumb to her charm and are obliged to admit that she has more than earned her keep.

In private, she holds strong, sometimes reactionary views, and her political perspective on the world is ultra-conservative; her outwardly sunny character has an iron and unforgiving streak. The Duke and Duchess of Windsor and the late Diana, Princess of Wales, viewed her with a reserve bordering on antipathy. The Prince of Wales, by contrast, her favourite grandchild, early fell under the spell of her charm, wit and steeliness of character. She is his closest confidant and a huge influence on his life.

She was covertly ambitious and, having reached the position of First Lady of Britain and its Empire, she quietly relished its trappings. She was no shrinking violet; public adulation was the oxygen of her existence, and now in the second half of her life she is never happier than when holding court as the centre of attention among a circle of adoring, witty acolytes. Early life in the bosom of a close, large, aristocratic but unpretentious family ensured that she was never overwhelmed by greatness, and she has retained throughout her life the knack of meeting people on their own level.

She will be remembered not for what she says, for her public utterances are few and she has almost never given an interview. She will be remembered for what she is and what she does and, as people might marvel at a great actress, they will wonder how she did it.

CHAPTER ONE

CHILDHOOD AND EARLY YEARS 1900-1913

July 1900 had been so hot that even the horses in the streets of London were wearing straw hats. But then came the August Bank Holiday and the rains. Play between Yorkshire and Essex at Harrogate was stopped, and the last day of Goodwood was marred by inglorious blustery showers and a disappointingly thin attendance.

OTHER CLOUDS WERE gathering, harbingers of the end of a long summer afternoon of imperial power, and of calamity to come. Victoria the Queen Empress was closeted at Osborne, in the 81st and last year of her life and the 64th of her reign. Tsar Nicholas II reigned in St Petersburg, Kaiser Wilhelm II in Berlin, Emperor Franz Joseph in Vienna, McKinley in the White House and Lord Salisbury in Downing Street.

Far away in South Africa, Victoria's troops were struggling, at great cost, to defend the empire against the Boers, causing those at home to entertain their first doubts of the merit of a world girdled in imperial red. In the first 14 months of campaigning the British death toll had reached 11,000, little more than a third of those from enemy action; more than 7,000 men died of dysentery, enteric fever and other diseases. Lord Kitchener sent an urgent request for 30,000 more mounted troops, and as a result virtually every trained soldier in Britain found himself on his way to the Cape.

Not all news from South Africa was bad. General Sir Redvers Buller relieved Ladysmith after 118 days of siege, and Lord Roberts broke the seven-month siege of Mafeking. In the wider world, Britain had lost its economic and industrial leadership to a United States revitalised after its Civil War and a Germany grown mighty with Bismarck's unification. Admiral von Tirpitz called for German mastery of the North Sea, and the yards of Bremen were set to building 38 new battleships in a direct challenge to the Royal Navy.

In that year Marconi took 'out a patent for wireless telegraphy, Claude Monet exhibited a painting of water lilies in his garden at Giverny, the premiere of Elgar's *Dream of Gerontius* was rapturously received in Birmingham, W.G. Grace retired from a cricketing career of 54,000 runs and Oscar Wilde died disgraced in Paris. But man had not yet stepped on the north or south poles, nor witnessed heavier-than-air flight. Fashion journals were hinting with rare boldness that the hemline might creep above the ankle.

The year witnessed the births of Spencer Tracy, Louis Armstrong, Aaron Copland, Heinrich Himmler, Lord Louis Mountbatten, the *Daily Express*, the Labour Party and a ninth child for Cecilia Nina, Lady Glamis, wife of the heir to the earldom of Strathmore, a title created by Charles II for the ancient Scottish family of Lyon.

At the age of 38, the childbearing days of Lady Glamis, a vicar's daughter related to the Duke of Portland, appeared to be over. Her firstborn, Violet, had died at the age of 11, but in the fashion of her times she had seven more living children, spanning the age range of 17 to seven.

Lady Glamis surprised one and all by giving birth, on 4 August 1900, to a healthy girl. The baby was christened Elizabeth after the Tudor queen, Angela because her father Claude Bowes Lyon, Lord Glamis, thought her an angel, and Marguerite after the common white daisy, her mother being a talented and knowledgeable gardener.

Where exactly the birth occurred is strangely mysterious. It was always assumed – and was stated on the birth certificate – that Elizabeth Angela Marguerite had been born at St Paul's Waldenbury, the Glamis family home near Hitchin in Hertfordshire. But on her 80th birthday Elizabeth let slip that she thought she had been born in London. It may have been in the family's town house at Grosvenor Gardens, or it may have been in an ambulance – she has never cared to elucidate further.

What is certain is that within days or even hours of the birth, while her father departed to an important cricket fixture in Scotland, mother and baby were shipped to St Paul's Waldenbury, a warm, rambling Queen Anne house with wonderfully secretive gardens hidden in the gentle folds of the Hertfordshire countryside.

▲ *Claude Monet's attempts to capture the myriad effects of light on water lilies helped pave the way to abstract art.*

▼ *Marconi, the wireless pioneer. 1901 saw the first successful trans-Atlantic radio message.*

Elizabeth found herself born into a large, close family and a world of unquestionable privilege. The Strathmores, relatively direct descendants of King Robert the Bruce, were old landowning aristocracy who had survived better than most the late Victorian agricultural depression which had forced so many of their class to sell up their stately homes and allow in an invasion of the nouveaux riches.

When Elizabeth was two her mother delivered another surprise – her tenth and positively her last child, a son named David. Lady Glamis called her late arrivals her "Little Benjamins", and because they were so distant in age from the rest of their siblings, and so close to each other, they became the inseparable, spirited, mischievous companions of an idyllic Edwardian childhood.

Unlike so many of her aristocratic contemporaries, Lady Glamis devoted much time to her children, breast-feeding them and taking personal charge of their early education. By the time she was seven, Elizabeth was well acquainted with all the familiar stories of the Bible and British history, and was becoming an accomplished pianist and dancer. She also, from the earliest age, had a natural poise. Visitors to the house would often remark on the polite ease with which they were greeted by this young child, and her ability to talk the hind legs off a donkey.

When Elizabeth was four Claude Glamis, on the death of his father, succeeded to the earldom of Strathmore, which brought with it the family seat of Glamis Castle, one of the oldest continuously inhabited houses in Scotland, and the London town house in St James's Square at which the newly elevated Earl entertained his peers and provided his youngest daughter with an early conduit into the highest of society. At the age of four she attended a children's party which numbered among its guests the nine-year-old Prince Albert, second son of the Prince of Wales. She thought he looked sad and offered him the cherries off her chocolate cake.

Elizabeth saw him again, from a distance, on 22 June 1911, when she and her sisters, in a fair state of excitement, stood outside Westminster Abbey to watch the procession of Albert's father to his coronation as King George V. The year held further thrills for an 11-year-old, when she and her brother made their first excursion abroad, travelling by sleeper train to visit their maternal grandmother at her villa in the hills above Florence. The vociferous Italians, so different from the dour Scots, made a lifelong impression on Elizabeth.

But all idylls end, and for Elizabeth the happy chapter of her childhood closed at the age of 12 when her brother left home for a

Where exactly the birth occurred is strangely mysterious. But on her 80th birthday Elizabeth let it slip that she thought she had been born in London. Either in the family's own house at Grosvenor Gardens, or it may have been in an ambulance — she has never cared to elucidate further.

▼ *Von Tirpitz's ambitions for Germany's Navy were disastrous for Anglo-German relations after 1900.*

At the age of four she attended a children's party which numbered among its guests the nine-year-old Prince Albert, second son of the Prince of Wales. She thought he looked sad and offered him the cherries off her chocolate cake.

Elizabeth in 1907.

boarding school in Broadstairs, in preparation for Eton. She was lonely, and consoled herself writing long letters. Although never a melancholy child, her mother thought that the gap left in Elizabeth's life by David's departure might usefully be filled by sending her daughter to school.

The chosen establishment was the Misses Birtwistle's Academy, a private day school in Sloane Street, which Elizabeth attended for several months and where she seemed happy enough, performing well in all her lessons except mathematics. Where she really excelled, however, was at her weekly dancing classes in Knightsbridge; to a girl in her position in society at the close of the Edwardian era, social graces counted for more than academic ability. After two terms, Elizabeth had had enough of school, and her French governess was summoned back from an extended holiday to resume charge of the girl's education.

The end of Elizabeth's childhood coincided with the end of an era for Britain, as indeed it did for the world at large. Victoria had been dead since 1901, but the age of material progress and transition her reign had embodied survival for another 13 years. The fecundity of 19th-century invention had continued into the early 20th century with the aeroplane, the motor car and the wireless. What came next, no Victorian in their worst nightmare could have envisaged.

FROM THE PAGES OF **THE TIMES**

BELFAST, MAY 31, 1911. In brilliant weather, and in the presence of thousands of spectators, the new White Star liner *Titanic* was successfully launched from the yard of Messrs. Harland and Wolff (Limited) a few minutes after noon this morning. Her sister ship, the *Olympic*, left for the Mersey in the afternoon, so that there was an opportunity of seeing almost side by side the two largest vessels afloat, which have between them, when loaded to their full draught of 34ft. 6in., an aggregate displacement of about 120,000 tons.

Some particulars of the vessels, with a description of their machinery, were given in The Times of Saturday. They are 882ft. 9in. long over all, or 850ft. over perpendiculars, and they have an extreme breadth of 92ft. 6in., with a depth moulded of 73ft. 6in. from the keel to the top of the beams of the bridge deck. Their gross tonnage is about 45,000 tons, 12,000 tons more than the *Mauretania*. They are propelled by three screws driven by two sets of four-crank triple-expansion reciprocating engines of 30,000 i.h.p., and an exhaust turbine giving 16,000 shaft h.p., and they are designed to maintain a continuous sea speed of 21 knots. Steam is supplied at a pressure of 215 lb. per square inch under natural draught by 29 boilers, having in all 159 furnaces.

LAUNCH OF THE TITANIC
Vessel successfully takes the water
(From our special correspondent)

The launching arrangements for the *Titanic* were similar to those in the case of the *Olympic* last October. In the hours immediately preceding the launch men were busily engaged in removing the shores, until the vessel was retained only by a hydraulic trigger, which was allowed to fall clear at the appropriate time by relieving the water pressure in the attached cylinder.

For checking the vessel's progress after she was afloat six anchors were provided, three on each side, connected with her hull by 7in. steel hawsers; and in addition there were two piles of cable drags, each weighing over 80 tons, placed in the bed of the river and attached to her by 8in. steel hawsers. Owing to the vessel being in a somewhat less advanced condition, the launching weight was less than that of the *Olympic*, being around 24,000 tons, as against 27,000 tons. The time occupied by her in sliding down the ways was 62 sec., and the maximum speed she attained was 12 knots. On becoming waterborne she was brought to a standstill in about her own length. The wave produced as her stem dropped into the water was much smaller than might have been expected considering the mass of the structure. The vessel was taken in charge by a number of tugs, which were waiting to tow her to the berth where she will be fitted out.

▲ The Strathmore family at St Paul's Waldenbury. Back row, left to right: Fergus, killed in action with the Black Watch at Loos in 1915; Jock, the second son; the Earl of Strathmore; Mary; the eldest son, Patrick; the third son Alexander, who died in 1911 aged 24; Front row: Rose, the second child; Lady Strathmore with, on her knee, David, who became Sir David Bowes Lyon; Elizabeth (perhaps encouraging a smile from her brother with her elbow); and Michael.

▶ Two-year-old Elizabeth poses on her birthday. Around her neck is a string of coral beads, which as Duchess of York she was to give to her infant elder daughter, the Queen, who in turn passed them on to her daughter, Anne, the Princess Royal.

▲ Elizabeth, when aged 11, visited her aunt, Lady Cavendish, and her grandmother the Duchess of Portland at the Villa Poggio Ponente at Bordighera. The trip was to bequeath her a lifelong love of Italy.

▼ *A scene captured on film by a visitor to Glamis Castle in the summer of 1909. In the castle's great hall Lady Elizabeth plays the princess in 16th-century-style fancy dress partnered by her seven-year-old brother, David, in jester costume. Like all children, they adored dressing-up.*

▲ ▼ *Elizabeth with her much-loved brother David, who called his sister 'Buffy' after early attempts to say 'Elizabuf'. Their happy childhood was in marked contrast to that of Elizabeth's future husband.*

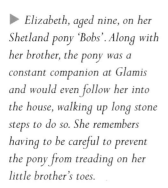 ▲ ▶ *Early friends: with a dog and a toy pony.*

▶ *Elizabeth, aged nine, on her Shetland pony 'Bobs'. Along with her brother, the pony was a constant companion at Glamis and would even follow her into the house, walking up long stone steps to do so. She remembers having to be careful to prevent the pony from treading on her little brother's toes.*

▶▶ *A seventh birthday portrait of Elizabeth, her hair worn in the fringe that would become so fashionable when she became a royal duchess.*

■ *Elizabeth at five years old. A year earlier her father had inherited the earldom of Strathmore, and from a mere 'honourable' she had become Lady Elizabeth, the first step on a titular ladder that would see her elevated beyond even the expectations of an earl's daughter. Also with the earldom came a fortune of some £250,000 (the equivalent at the end of the century being nigh on seven figures) and Glamis Castle, beautifully situated in the shadow of the Grampian Mountains. This meant summer holidays in Scotland, a taste for which remains with Elizabeth to this day. Here also was born her lifelong love of fishing, which she first took up as a palatable alternative to shooting. For Elizabeth the annual trip to Glamis was a homecoming — not only to her Scottish roots, but also to the fabulous outdoors of woods and heather in which she and her brother would ride and play, accompanied by a huge, ever-changing menagerie of dogs, cats, tortoises, ponies and pet doves. The castle itself was a forbidding place, believed by many to be the most haunted residence in the British Isles — 'Spooky but marvellous,' the Queen Mother recalls.*

◀ *George V, seen here on the day of his coronation, 22 June 1911. The Strathmores had had little to do with the court of Edward VII, whose racy and fashionable entourage was not to their taste. But the accession of George V bred a court of a very different tone, which would eventually bring royalty once again to Glamis Castle, through their neighbour, the Countess of Airlie, lady-in-waiting to the new queen.*

▼ *Lord Salisbury, Tory Prime Minister in 1900, warned of a 'terrible effort of mutual destruction' should Europe's growing militarism not be curbed.*

▲ *Keir Hardie was sent out to work at seven years old and by the age of ten was toiling down the mines. He was elected as an Independent Labour MP in 1892 and subsequently became one of the founders of the Parliamentary Labour Party. Although he had the zeal of a prophet and never sold out to the Establishment during his long battle to win 'equality, freedom and triumphant self-reliance' for the working class, he was at the same time an accomplished parliamentary tactician.*

CHAPTER TWO

THE GREAT WAR 1914–1918

Beneath the flat, waving cornfields of Belgium and northern France lie the remains of one million sons of Britain and her empire. Half are buried under the simple headstones of the Commonwealth War Graves Commission; the names of the other half scroll endlessly down the brooding memorials of Arras, Thiepval and elsewhere. They are the lost 500,000 who perished in the mud of the trenches and who were never found.

THE GREAT WAR ROBBED Britain of an entire generation, many of them virgin soldiers who died before they had really lived. In almost every street in the land there was at least one house with its blinds drawn in mourning, and every mother, as she saw the telegraph boy pedal into view, prayed that his sorry tidings were bound for some other door.

Sixty years of Anglo-German antagonism and jockeying for economic and political dominance in Europe came to its inevitable head on 4 August 1914. It was Elizabeth Bowes Lyon's 14th birthday, celebrated by a visit with her parents to a West End show at the London Coliseum to see Charles Hawtrey. That same evening her future father-in-law King George V wrote in his diary: "I held a Council at 10.45 to declare war with Germany. It is a terrible catastrophe, but it is not our fault. An enormous crowd collected outside the Palace; we went on the balcony both before and after dinner."

Propelled by a sense of patriotism, comradeship, duty and adventure, young men hastened to enlist in what they believed

▲ *The Prince of Wales, cutting a somewhat slight figure, marches from Buckingham Palace at the outbreak of war.*

▼ *Crowds gather outside Buckingham Palace to hear the Declaration of War by the King, 4 August 1914.*

would be a brief and decisive encounter lasting until shortly before Christmas. They were not to know then that it would develop into history's first mass slaughter of conscript armies or that Germany would ultimately be defeated by economic blockade as much as by attrition in the trenches of the Western Front.

It was a defining moment of the century – and in the life of the Strathmore family. Elizabeth's three eldest surviving brothers Patrick, Jock and Fergus (another, Alexander, had died young and somewhat mysteriously in 1911) hurried to rejoin their regiment, the Black Watch. A fourth brother, Michael, abandoned his studies at Magdalen College, Oxford, and immediately enlisted in the Royal Scots.

Before embarking for France, two brothers made a dash for the altar, Jock marrying the majestically named Hon Fenella Hepburn-Stuart-Forbes-Trefusis, Fergus settling for a single hyphen in Lady Christian Dawson-Damer.

The London house was closed up and the Strathmores retreated to the family seat at Glamis Castle, a romantic red sandstone pile set in a broad valley of Angus in the hinterland of Dundee. Reeking of history and legend, its atmosphere permeated Elizabeth from an early age. Glamis is supposedly the setting used by Shakespeare for Macbeth's murder of King Duncan. More historically sound are its links with previous occupants and visitors from Mary, Queen of Scots, to those principal combatants of the 1745 Jacobite rebellion, Bonnie Prince Charlie and the Duke of Cumberland, butcher of Culloden. Glamis is as much a shrine to the Stuarts as it is to Hanoverian history.

Some of Glamis' legends are less comfortably romantic, as in the unproven tale of a previous rightful Strathmore heir of the early 19th century, born hideously deformed, who was said to have been walled up in a dungeon for the entirety of his long life. An estate worker who caught an accidental glimpse of the Monster of Glamis was reputedly dismissed on the spot without explanation and given a sum of money and a one-way passage to America. It was an uncomfortable reminder of genetic imperfection when, in 1986, two of Elizabeth's nieces, daughters of her brother Jock and both presumed dead, were discovered as long-term residents of a mental institution in the south of England. Their identity established, Elizabeth chose not to visit them; instead she sent a cheque to a mental health charity.

On the outbreak of war Lady Strathmore, a woman of strong Christian principles and a sense of noblesse oblige, opened Glamis as a convalescent home equipped with 16 beds, although she had to wait until Christmas to receive her first patients invalided home from the trenches. Elizabeth became hospital dogsbody, her first tasks being to knit comforters and to crumple up tissue paper as lining for sleeping bags.

In September 1915 Fergus came home on leave to see his two-month old daughter for the first time. Three days after his return to France he was killed in action at the Battle of Loos, aged only 26. Lady Strathmore, having already lost two of her children, was broken by the news. She became a semi-invalid and effectively withdrew from her hospital, leaving its running to her daughters Rose, a qualified nursing sister, and Elizabeth.

Despite an age gap of 11 years, the death of Fergus had an equally deep, if different, effect on Elizabeth. From her earliest years she had been a bright, open and easy-going character, full of gaiety and mischief and often displaying a maturity beyond her years, the result of an upbringing within a large and close family and surrounded by elder brothers. She was undoubtedly affected by the death of her brother Alexander when she was 11, but the death of Fergus was a far greater watershed, and the effect it had on her mother left a deep and permanent impression. Whilst outwardly she retained her beguiling charm, somewhere behind those blue eyes a shutter came down, and she became particularly adept at keeping her private thoughts to herself, deftly sidestepping any probing, argument or controversy in conversation or unpleasantness in her daily life. A fair degree of iron had entered her soul.

For an aristocratic teenager born to privilege, looking after 16 wounded soldiers in her own dining room was a humbling and levelling experience, which can only have served to hone the common touch she displayed with such aplomb in her later public life. For the next four years, she gave the soldiers her constant attention. She had no formal nursing training, but she wrote their letters, fetched their tobacco from the village shop, played them at whist, led them in spirit-raising sing-songs and even dressed up her brother David as a girl and introduced him round the ward as a long-lost cousin. Most of all she talked to them, a surrogate for distant wives, mothers, daughters or sweethearts. One of the men she tended wrote of her: "She had the loveliest eyes, expressive and eloquent eyes, and a very taking way of knitting her forehead when speaking ... that sweet, quiet voice, that hesitating yet open way of speaking. For all her 15 years she was womanly, kind-hearted and sympathetic."

The death of a son in action had cast a heavy pall over Glamis, as it did over countless homes of every social class. Early in 1917 the

For an aristocratic teenager born to privilege, looking after 16 wounded soldiers in her own dining room was a humbling and levelling experience, which can only have served to hone the common touch she displayed in later life.

▼ *'Kitchener's Army' training in Hyde Park. His famous 'Your Country Needs You' call recruited thousands.*

An Irish rebel, wounded in the Easter Rising of 1916, is brought out of the Dublin Post Office following the surrender to British troops.

feared telegraph boy pedalled up to the castle with news that another Bowes Lyon boy, Michael, was missing in action, presumed killed. But the report was unduly pessimistic; after an agonising three months, word reached Scotland that he had in fact been wounded and taken prisoner and had been found alive in a prison hospital in Germany.

Amid the bleakness of the war there was an outburst of rejoicing at Glamis. It was followed by an even greater one when, after a seemingly endless wait for his repatriation, Michael turned up at Dundee railway station one fine day in 1919. Many years later, Queen Elizabeth would take a particular pleasure in being invited to become Colonel-in-Chief of the Black Watch, with her granddaughter Anne in the same honorary position with the Royal Scots.

The war continued in its merciless slaughter, medieval in its use of human cannon fodder yet simultaneously, with its employment of tanks, barbed wire, murderously efficient machine guns and, at sea, submarines, the first great technological conflict. The replacement of Sir John French by Sir Douglas Haig as Commander-in-Chief failed to alter the conflict's essential nature – two vast armies bogged down in a war of attrition, where an advance of a mile could cost hundreds of thousands of lives.

Still to come were the great battles of Arras, Paschendale and the Somme, with their mind-numbing numbers of dead. Heavy artillery standing wheel-to-wheel for 18 miles, creating a noise that shattered eardrums and minds and could be heard across the Channel in Kent, failed to soften up the exceptionally well dug-in Germans or to flatten the barbed wire on which thousands of infantrymen became entangled in the direct line of enemy machine gunners.

Those back home were only dimly aware of true conditions at the front. Newspapers were censored, there was no television that today brings war into the living room and somehow sanitises it, and those soldiers returning on leave were often too shocked, too numbed by the experience to talk about it to their families.

At Glamis as elsewhere, the war dominated life and other historic events of the time seemed sideshows by comparison. In 1917 the Bolshevik revolution in Russia toppled Queen Victoria's granddaughter Alex and her husband Tsar Nicholas II. Their entire family was murdered, their bodies thrown down a mineshaft. They had to await the end of more than seven decades of Soviet-dominated communist rule before receiving their rightful Christian burial in the Cathedral of Peter and Paul in St Petersburg, when

Elizabeth was in her 98th year.

At Easter 1916, the eternal thorn of Ireland pricked the British side in an uprising at the General Post Office in Dublin that led to civil war, partition, eventual independence for the south and a seemingly insoluble political situation in the north. Ireland, like most other political issues of the real world, was far too tangled a thicket for Elizabeth ever to voice an opinion upon in public.

For the latter part of the war Elizabeth, still a mere teenager, found herself more or less in charge of the Glamis hospital. Her mother remained deeply affected by the loss of Fergus while her sister Rose had fallen for marriage to the Hon William Leveson-Gower, a relative of the Duke of Sutherland. That family enjoyed an especially fearsome reputation for driving crofter tenant farmers off their land during the long and shameful period of the Highland Clearances which followed the extinction of the Jacobite cause, and the old Highland way of life, at the Battle of Culloden in 1746.

It was 1919 before the last patients left Glamis, piling the Strathmores – and Elizabeth in particular – with parting gifts. As the last of them disappeared down the long castle drive, the words of *Goodbye Dolly I Must Leave You* wafted back on the breeze.

The war, which had cost an estimated ten million lives worldwide, was over; at Versailles the peace treaty was being horse-

Amid the bleakness of the war there was an outburst of rejoicing at Glamis. It was followed by an even greater one when, after a seemingly endless wait for his repatriation, Michael turned up at Dundee railway station one fine day in 1919.

FROM THE PAGES OF **THE  TIMES**

HOW TO BE USEFUL IN WAR-TIME

AUGUST 6, 1914. We are receiving a constant stream of letters containing suggestions for personal conduct or useful action in the national emergency. We publish a selection from them below. They vary, no doubt, in value and publication does not imply endorsement of any particular suggestion. But they all reflect the intense interest and desire to help which animates the whole population, and they will, we hope, encourage the spirit of duty, unselfishness, restraint, and consideration for others which it behoves us all to cherish to the utmost. There are some simple things that all can do and others that all can avoid.

To the Editor of the Times Sir, – First and foremost – Keep your heads. Be calm. Go about your ordinary business quietly and soberly. Do not indulge in excitement or foolish demonstrations. Secondly – Think of others more than you are wont to do. Think of your duty to your neighbour. Think of the common weal. Remember those who are worse off than yourself. Pay punctually what you owe, especially to your poorest creditors, such as washerwomen and charwomen. If you are an employer think of your employed. Give them work and wages as long as you can, and work short time rather than close down.

To the Editor of the Times Sir, – When I went to the Army and Navy Stores yesterday I was disgusted to see hundreds of people whom one cannot dignify by calling men and women, laying in tons of provisions. It is a time of war, and we are fighting for our existence as a nation. Surely the Government ought to confiscate these private stores, and fine and imprison the selfish brutes who are hoarding them.

To the Editor of the the Times Sir, – Many civilians who are too old to volunteer are asking how by personal service they can help their country. May I suggest that for the next few weeks they could not do a greater service than help to gather in the crops, which in many parts of the country are heavier than usual. There will be scarcely a rural parish in England which will not have lost some of its harvesters, and every sack of wheat safely gathered in will enable at least two men in the fighting line, whether on sea or land, to be kept there for thirty days.

The Rev. James Redfearn writes from Maindee, Newport, Mon. – "I suggest that the breweries and distilleries be closed down and the grain used for food. It is vastly more important that the millions of our people have cheap bread than beer."

Women gained far more than the vote from the war. They earned good wages, while the working conditions in the factories gave them the freedom to cut their hair short and to wear dress more suited to the traditionally masculine activities they undertook.

▼ *Demonstrators being kept out of the first camp of the Regular IRA after the Great War.*

traded that would sow the seeds of the next world war in its excessive punishment of a defeated Germany. The death toll of the conflict was monstrous, yet worse was immediately to follow; the global influenza epidemic of 1918-19 killed an estimated 20 million.

The world was now a different place, Britain a different country. Four years of fighting had supposedly united a nation and broken down old class barriers. If that was true it was neither immediately nor dramatically apparent in Elizabeth's stratum of society, which slipped with relative ease back into its old pre-war life. What the war did more than anything else to British society, apart from robbing it of a whole generation of young men, was to advance hugely the cause of women.

For all the heroic acts of suffragettes, chaining themselves to the railings of Downing Street or throwing themselves under King George V's horse at the Derby, it was the First World War which enabled them to achieve their aims. Since 1915 women had been working in the munitions factories, driving lorries, toiling in the land army, even serving in auxiliary posts in the Army and Navy. Their worth to the economic life of the country could no longer be denied, and in 1918 the parliamentary bill giving women over 30 the vote passed unopposed into law.

In the election of 1918 which immediately followed the armistice, the voters of Dublin – still part of the United Kingdom – elected Westminster's first woman MP. But as the winning candidate, Countess Markievicz, was a Sinn Fein Irish nationalist she refused to take the oath of allegiance to the Crown, and was thereby prevented from taking her seat in the Commons. Sinn Fein MPs elected in Northern Ireland were adopting precisely the same stance in 1997. Nancy Astor, who won Plymouth for the Conservatives in the 1919 election, was the first woman actually to take her seat.

Women gained far more than the vote from the war. They earned good wages, and the working conditions in the factories gave them the freedom to cut their hair short, and to wear dress more suited to the traditionally masculine activities they undertook. In 1914 a woman's hem touched the ground; by the time of the Armistice it had crept halfway up the calf. And in 1916, for the first time, there appeared on the market a new undergarment to replace the old-fashioned camisole and to give moral support in the stress of war: the brassiere had arrived.

◄ *Queen Mary surrounded by her family, with the young Elizabeth standing behind her to the right, next to her father the Earl of Strathmore.*

▼ *The Royal Family were deeply shocked by the savage deaths of their Russian cousins, the family of the Romanov Tsar of Russia. However, there was a touch of guilt amongst the grief. The year before, when Prime Minister Lloyd George had supported the Russian provisional government's request for Britain to grant the Tsar and his family asylum, the King at first agreed to send a cruiser to fetch them to safety in England but then reneged. Afraid of stirring up revolutionary forces at home during a critical period in the war, he abandoned 'dear Nicky' to his fate. After the war British troops would be sent to Russia in an unsuccessful attempt to oust the new Bolshevik regime.*

▶ *Elizabeth flanked by her brother, Lord Glamis, and her father the Earl of Strathmore, in a picture taken shortly before her wedding. The earl was extremely fond of his moustache and used to make a great show of parting it in order to kiss his younger children.*

▼ ▶▶ *Pictures in the Bowes Lyon family album taken after the Great War show an Elizabeth still close to her childhood companion, brother David, but also older and wiser. Her wartime duties and the loss of her brother Fergus had forced her to grow up quickly. Nevertheless, she retained her humour and her warmth, and her cheerfulness made her very popular with the convalescing soldiers at Glamis — so much so that one man said that when he returned to the front he would wear a label reading, 'Please return to Glamis', in case he was injured again.*

▶ 'What passing-bells for these who die as cattle?' A scene from the carnage at Hell Fire Corner, Ypres, in 1914.

▼ A British ammunition column struggles through the thick mud on the Western Front.

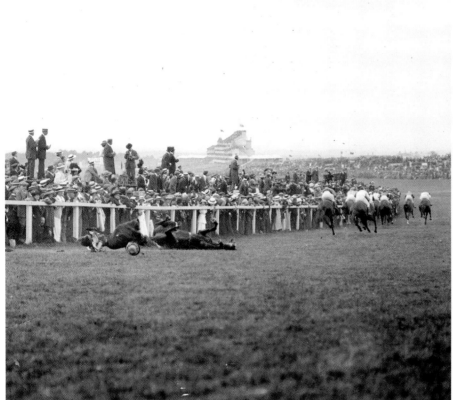

■ *The election of Nancy Astor (above) in 1919 marked a breakthrough in women's political rights. Her success was in contrast to the pre-war efforts of such as Emily Davidson (left), who threw herself under the king's horse in the Derby and Mrs Purdy (below).*

▶ The war transformed the lives of women in Britain. With millions of men needed for the attritional warfare in France, women were welcomed into jobs previously the strict preserve of men. Even that bastion of conservatism, Harrods, found itself employing a woman commissionaire.

▼ Agriculture as much as industry saw women employed for the first time in huge numbers during the war. The picture shows a novelty for 1917: a women farmers' competition.

▼ ▶ Fashions at Ascot and Henley in 1914. The seeming solidity of the Edwardian world was shattered by the horrors of the Great War.

CHAPTER THREE

COURTSHIP AND MARRIAGE 1919–1923

Among the upper-class smart set of 1920s London,

Lady Elizabeth Bowes Lyon stood out from the crowd,

not so much through fashion-plate looks – which she did

not possess – as by subtler qualities of womanhood.

ACLOSE OBSERVER OF HER in those years was Mabell, Countess of Airlie, who described her thus: "She was very unlike the cocktail-drinking, chain-smoking girls who came to be regarded as typical of the 1920s. Her radiant vitality and a blending of gaiety, kindness and sincerity made her irresistible to men. One knew instinctively that she was a girl who would find real happiness only in marriage and motherhood."

Penelope Mortimer, a much more recent biographer, drew a sharp distinction between the appeal of Elizabeth and that of Diana, Princess of Wales. The most formidable characteristic of the young – and not so young – Elizabeth was sexuality.

Mortimer wrote: "I am not suggesting that as either Duchess of York or as Queen she invited lovers to bed. On the contrary. Rigid moral principles often leave huge reserves of excess energy available for other purposes, as many saints, martyrs and philanthropists demonstrate. All I suggest is that the power which transformed Prince Albert from an inarticulate nobody into a man of some stature, hypnotised the media and eventually reinstated the throne in the public's fantasy was essentially – if the term is preferable – female."

Mortimer, on the other hand, regarded Diana as merely sexy, "an ephemeral and less

▲ *Elizabeth shopping in London before her marriage to the Duke of York.*

▼ *The bride wore ivory chiffon moiré with pearls and silver thread. Her sleeves were of Nottingham lace, and the train, which used to be her mother's, was of point de Flandres lace on tulle.*

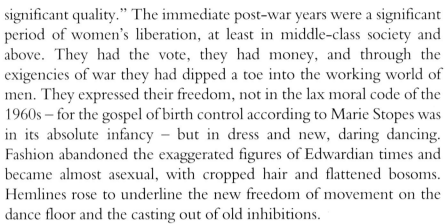

significant quality." The immediate post-war years were a significant period of women's liberation, at least in middle-class society and above. They had the vote, they had money, and through the exigencies of war they had dipped a toe into the working world of men. They expressed their freedom, not in the lax moral code of the 1960s – for the gospel of birth control according to Marie Stopes was in its absolute infancy – but in dress and new, daring dancing. Fashion abandoned the exaggerated figures of Edwardian times and became almost asexual, with cropped hair and flattened bosoms. Hemlines rose to underline the new freedom of movement on the dance floor and the casting out of old inhibitions.

Elizabeth was formally launched into society at the age of 18, when her mother gave the traditional coming-out dance for her. She was small, mildly flirtatious and, in the overused term of the times, "dainty". She dressed, according to Mabell Airlie, more picturesquely than fashionably.

She had no real need of a formal introduction into high society for she was part of it already. In 1919 she was a bridesmaid to Lady Lavinia Spencer, a forebear of Diana, at her wedding at Althorp, and in 1922 she performed the same role at the wedding of Princess Mary, King George V's only daughter, to Viscount Lascelles.

How many male hearts she broke during her brief years between coming-out and marriage we shall never know. There is no real evidence to suggest that she gave her heart to anyone in that period, although she had no shortage of pursuers. One such was Major James Stuart, a dashing war hero who was briefly equerry to Prince Albert, newly created Duke of York. When his ardour became too manifest, he found himself mysteriously relieved of his royal duties and sent instead to toil anonymously in the oilfields of Oklahoma.

At a dance in Grosvenor Square in 1920, Elizabeth again found herself in the company of her occasional childhood friend Prince Albert, the King's second son, Bertie to his family. Bertie's interest was kindled; that autumn he motored over from Balmoral to Glamis to visit her, as he was to do on many more occasions.

But the traffic was decidedly one-way; Elizabeth was still young and exceedingly cautious, and Bertie's personality fell somewhat short of magnetic. Besides, the Strathmores were the last people to be impressed by royal connections; Elizabeth's father had been disgusted by the louche lifestyle of Edward VII, although he agreed that Bertie himself seemed a perfectly decent chap.

Then Queen Mary took a hand. Her second son talked so much of young Elizabeth that the formidable old Dane drove to Glamis to see for herself. She was deeply impressed by the way Elizabeth deputised for her mother, who was ill, and confided in a friend that the Bowes Lyon girl might be the perfect bride – not for Bertie but for his elder brother the Prince of Wales. The Queen was tempted to matchmake, but wisely kept her own counsel. Elizabeth, given her socially ambitious nature, briefly considered the heir to the throne as a marriage prospect, but he was a flawed character and there is no evidence that the pair ever took more than a passing interest in each other.

▲ *The moment Elizabeth's engagement was announced, she was inundated with requests to sit for society artists.*

Bertie was nothing if not persistent. With his parents' backing, he set about wearing down Elizabeth's resistance, although at least two of his proposals of marriage were rejected. To cover Elizabeth's uncertainty it was put about that, like Diana in later years, she was terrified of the prospect of a public life. That, of course, was perfectly true, if not the whole truth. Eventually, in January 1923, Bertie was invited to spend the weekend with the Strathmores at St Paul's Waldenbury, a house with which he had become increasingly familiar. On the Sunday morning he and Elizabeth were excused church, an enormous concession in such a God-fearing household; they went for a walk in the garden, and returned engaged. The Duke of York immediately sent a telegram in prearranged code to his father at Sandringham: "All right. Bertie."

Sir Henry "Chips" Channon, the leading diarist and social commentator of the day, noted on hearing the news: "We have all hoped, waited, so long for this romance to prosper, that we had begun to despair that she would ever accept him. He has been the most ardent of wooers; he is the luckiest of men." Elizabeth, he wrote, was "more gentle, lovely and exquisite than any woman alive." Channon was by no means the last homosexual to fawn over Elizabeth.

In 1923 the marriage of a prince to a commoner was still exceedingly rare; indeed, it had been almost unknown since Henry VIII married four of them – Anne Boleyn, Jane Seymour, Catherine Howard and Catherine Parr. It was also the first time since Richard II in 1382 that a prince was to be married in Westminster Abbey; royal weddings, even in the High Victorian era, had been essentially private family affairs conducted in royal chapels at Windsor or St James's Palace.

But King George V decreed that the wedding of Bertie and Elizabeth, on 26 April 1923, should be a public spectacle to brighten the postwar depression, just as the marriage of Princess Elizabeth to Lt Philip Mountbatten would be in 1947. The groom wore the

▼ *April 1923: the King and his sons leaving Windsor Castle, where they spent the Easter holidays, for a ride in the Great Park. The Prince of Wales is in front with his father, and behind are the Duke of York (left), Prince Henry (centre) and Prince George.*

Bertie was nothing if not persistent. With his parents' backing, he set about wearing down Elizabeth's resistance, although at least two of his proposals of marriage were rejected.

▶▶ *The new bride took to her new public role with becoming and typical panache. Here, in June 1923, she is presented with a bouquet at Richmond Royal Horse Show.*

uniform of a Group Captain of the Royal Air Force, a singular honour for an armed service formed only five years previously in the last months of the war. The bride wore a dress of ivory chiffon with a train of point de Flandres lace, which she keeps to this day in a wardrobe at Clarence House.

The ceremony attracted tens of thousands of spectators to London, but the infant British Broadcasting Company, created the previous year to promote the new medium of wireless, was refused permission by the Dean and Chapter of the Abbey to relay the service to the nation on the grounds that disrespectful citizens might listen to it in pubs with their hats on.

On the morning of the wedding, *The Times* commented: "In the public mind, Lady Elizabeth Bowes Lyon is probably all the more welcome an addition to the Royal Family because the public knows practically nothing about her."

What the public now knows about her, they know second-hand. Shortly before her wedding she agreed to be interviewed by a reporter from the *Daily Sketch*, the most popular tabloid newspaper of its day. She told him a few meaningless pleasantries and showed him her engagement ring. But the harmless exchange earned the stern disapproval of her future father-in-law. Remarkably, it was the last interview she ever gave.

FROM THE PAGES OF THE TIMES

JANUARY 16, 1923. It is with the greatest pleasure that The King and Queen announce the betrothal of Their beloved son the Duke of York to the Lady Elizabeth Bowes Lyon, daughter of the Earl and Countess of Strathmore and Kinghorne, to which union The King has gladly given His Consent. The announcement followed the arrival of the Duke of York at Sandringham yesterday.

The Duke of York is perhaps best known for the practical interest which he takes in welfare work. The nation has also not been slow to mark how efficiently he has helped his brother, the Prince of Wales, in fulfilling those varied duties of the Royal House which have become much more numerous and exacting than they were in the less complex age of Queen Victoria. Last October, he represented his parents at the Coronation of the King and Queen of Rumania, where he made a great impression by the modest grace and unaffected friendliness of his bearing. Before that he had to his credit a remarkable record of public service at home. The outbreak of war found him a midshipman in HMS *Collingwood*, and though, to his lasting grief, he was laid aside by two periods of disabling illness, he rejoined his ship in time for the Battle of Jutland, where he was

DUKE OF YORK BETROTHED. LADY ELIZABETH BOWES LYON.
The following announcement was made in the Court Circular last evening:

commended for his services.

It is significant that when he went to Cambridge in 1919 his studies were in History, Economics and Civics. He had already demonstrated his interest in the practical problems of industry, and by visits, often incognito, to factories, works, collieries and shipyards. In 1921, he invited 400 boys, half from the great public schools and half from purely working-class homes, to join in the friendly intercourse of a sea-side camp. The experiment was so great a success that he repeated it last summer.

His Royal Highness Prince Albert Frederick Arthur George, Duke of York, Earl of Inverness, and Baron Killarney, the second son of the King and Queen, was born at York Cottage, Sandringham, on December 14, 1895.

Lady Elizabeth Angela Marguerite Bowes Lyon is the fourth daughter of the Earl and Countess of Strathmore and Kinghorne. The family has played a considerable part in history. Lady Elizabeth Bowes Lyon was one of the bridesmaids to Princess Mary, of whom she is one of the most intimate friends. She is high-spirited, clever and accomplished as well as beautiful, and for some time past has been made welcome in Royal circles.

◀ ▲ At 11.12 am on 26 April 1923, for the last time as a single woman, Lady Elizabeth steps out of her family house at 17 Bruton Street, Mayfair, on her way to her wedding. A footman stands either side of her, and her father waits in the state landau. Her flowers were also in the carriage. They included sprigs of white heather from Scotland and white roses to signify the Duchy of York. As she entered Westminster Abbey she placed them on the tomb of the Unknown Soldier.

▲ The first royal marriage to be celebrated in Westminster Abbey since the future Richard II married Anne of Bohemia there 541 years previously. The King had asked for the ceremony to be kept as simple as possible without any undue expense, but the setting, the vestments and the uniforms, with the sun striking through the stained glass windows, made it a magnificent occasion. Perhaps inevitably, the wedding increased speculation about the marriage plans of Bertie's brother, the Prince of Wales.

◀ ▲ *After the wedding the newly married couple made an appearance on the balcony at Buckingham Palace. The heavy drape gives the picture a slightly sombre air. This photograph must have been taken from scaffolding in front and slightly to the right of the Palace, not from* the Victoria Memorial, as would be the case today.

▶▶ *The Duke and Duchess of York on their honeymoon in April 1923.*

▲ ▶ *The formal wedding group at Buckingham Palace. With the royal couple are* the Earl and Countess of Strathmore and King George V and Queen Mary.

◀ *The newlyweds' royal duties started almost immediately after their wedding. Here they are shown visiting Cheyne Hospital for Children in July 1923.*

▼ ▶ *The Royal Family was punctilious in the observance of its duties towards wounded ex-servicemen. (Right) The Duchess presides over a Christmas party, held in 1923 at Buckingham Palace under the auspices of the Not Forgotten Association. (Below) at a garden party earlier that year.*

▲ *A shooting party in August 1923, as the two families recently united by marriage get to know each other better. The picture shows, from left to right: Lord Doune and The Hon. Bruce Ogilvy, family friends; David Bowes Lyon, Elizabeth's youngest brother and childhood companion; the Prince of Wales; the new Duchess of York; her father, the Earl of Strathmore; Elizabeth's sister, Rose, by then Lady Leveson-Gower; and the Duke of York.*

▶▶ *Elizabeth arriving on the course at Royal Ascot in 1924.*

CHAPTER FOUR

FAMILY LIFE 1924 - 1935

King George V may have been irked at his future daughter-in-law giving an interview to the newspapers but in every other respect he was hopelessly charmed by her. His greatest concession was to forgive her notorious unpunctuality which so jarred with his own life of stultifyingly precise order. On one occasion, when she committed the cardinal sin of arriving at Sandringham two minutes late for dinner, the King melted: "My dear, we must have sat down two minutes early."

SOON AFTER THE MARRIAGE the King wrote to Bertie: "The better I know, and the more I see, of your dear little wife, the more charming I think she is, and everyone falls in love with her here." Elizabeth, although high-born and with a cut-glass Mayfair accent despite her Scottish roots, was unused to the stiff court ways of King George and Queen Mary. But she was a quick learner with a full quiver of social skills, and she took to her new role as a royal daughter-in-law with ease and with a relish that suggested an innate ambition for high position.

The couple determined to build a strong and close family life – she because she was used to it, he because he had been deprived of it. After the stern regulated existence of Sandringham under a father who was the soul of kindness to everyone but his own children, marriage, freedom, a good woman and his own home were bliss to Bertie.

David, Prince of Wales, was a glamorous but flawed individual who developed a taste for other men's wives. Henry, Duke of Gloucester, was a dim and unimaginative military dunce whom his brothers nicknamed The Unknown Soldier. And George, Duke of Kent, was a bisexual with a drug habit who knew little of the world outside nightclubs.

▼ *In October 1923, the Duchess accompanied her husband to Belgrade for the christening of Prince Peter of Yugoslavia. Whatever the pomp of the occasion , the vast interconnecting network of European royalty it brought together was not to endure for much longer.*

They had much in common. Both had that well-developed sense of noblesse oblige, both had a strong and simple religious faith, and although Bertie had his weaknesses he was essentially a steady and steadfast character, if given to occasional bouts of temper, a bad stammer and chain-smoking.

He was certainly more promising material than any of his three surviving brothers (the epileptic Prince John had died at the age of 13). David, Prince of Wales, was a glamorous but flawed individual who developed a taste for other men's wives. Henry, Duke of Gloucester, was a dim and unimaginative military dunce whom his brothers nicknamed The Unknown Soldier. And George, Duke of Kent, was a bisexual with a drug habit who knew little of the world outside nightclubs.

Elizabeth used her own confidence to build that of her husband. She sent him to Lionel Logue, an Australian speech therapist practising in Harley Street, who worked wonders on Bertie's stammer. After his first encounter with his new patient, Logue wrote: "He entered my consulting room at three o'clock in the afternoon, a slim, quiet man with tired eyes and all the outward symptoms of the man upon whom habitual speech defect had begun to set the sign. When he left at five o'clock, you could see there was hope once more in his heart."

Elizabeth's confidence-building had other effects. In 1926 Bertie, always a keen tennis player, progressed as far as the men's doubles at that year's Wimbledon championships.

Marriage into the Royal Family meant a round of public duties, although for the Yorks they were never unduly arduous. Elizabeth's first overseas engagement came soon after her wedding in 1923, when she and Bertie represented the King at the christening of the infant Prince Peter of Yugoslavia in Belgrade. The full splendour of Balkan royalty was laid forth for the occasion, intended as a celebration of the assured succession of the House of Karageorgevic on the throne of the new Triune Kingdom of the Serbs, Croats and Slovenes.

For the Duchess of York, it was her first opportunity to meet some of the more distant branches of the family she had married into. The indefatigable Queen Marie of Romania constantly emphasised her

family connection with Britain, and boasted at the solidarity of the Balkan monarchies she had sought to unite through a web of family alliances.

Sir John Wheeler-Bennett, George VI's official biographer, wrote: "The gift of futurity of vision is perhaps never one to be desired, but had it been available to any of the participants, the effect might well have been one of gloom." Of the vast assemblage of European monarchy gathered on that occasion, Elizabeth has outlasted them all. Such is the turbulent history of Europe that her husband apart, every other royal guest at that christening was deposed, exiled or met a violent death.

Death of a different if equally violent kind confronted Elizabeth in 1925 when she and Bertie took a four-month safari holiday in Kenya. In the fashion of the times, they slaughtered everything in sight. Bertie bagged his first elephant. Elizabeth's personal tally ran to a rhinoceros, buffalo, waterbuck, oryx, Grant's gazelle, antelope, hartebeest, steinbuck, waterhog and a jackal.

On 21 April the following year, Elizabeth gave birth by Caesarean section to her first child at 17 Bruton Street, Mayfair, one of the Strathmores' London homes. There was mild disappointment from the King and Queen that their first grandchild, christened Elizabeth Alexandra Mary, was not a boy, but it was a minor matter

▲ The Wall Street crash of 1929 precipitated economic collapse across the globe and did much to destabilize a Europe still grappling with the turbulent aftermath of war.

FROM THE PAGES OF THE TIMES

THE GENERAL STRIKE

MAY 5, 1926. A wide response was made yesterday throughout the country to the call of those Unions which had been ordered by the T.U.C. to bring out their members. Railway workers stopped generally, though at Hull railway clerks are reported to have resumed duty, confining themselves to their ordinary work, and protested against the strike. Commercial road transport was only partially suspended. In London the tramways services were stopped. The printing industry is practically at a standstill, but lithographers have not been withdrawn, and compositors in London have not received instructions to strike. Large numbers of building operatives, other than those working on housing, came out.

The situation in the engineering trades was confused; men in some districts stopped while in others they continued to work. There was no interference with new construction in the ship building yards, but some of the men engaged on repair work joined in the strike.

Food – Supplies of milk and fish brought into Kings Cross, Euston and Paddington were successfully distributed from the Hyde Park Depot and stations. The Milk & Food Controller expects it will be possible to maintain a satisfactory supply of milk to hospitals, institutions, schools, hotels, restaurants and private consumers. Smithfield market has distributed 5,000 tons of meat since Monday. Mails – Efforts will be made to forward by means of road transport the mails already shown as due to be dispatched shortly from London. The position is uncertain and the facilities may have to be limited to mails for America, India and Africa.

Full tram and bus services were running yesterday at Bristol, Lincoln, Southampton, Aldershot, Bournmouth and Isle-of-Wight, and partial services in Edinburgh, Glasgow, Liverpool, Leeds, Northampton, Cardiff, Portsmouth, Dover, N. Derbyshire and Monmouthshire. Evening papers appeared at Bristol, Southampton, several Lancashire towns and Edinburgh. Road and Rail Transport – There was no railway passenger transport in London yesterday except a few suburban trains. Every available form of transport was used. A few independent omnibuses were running, but by the evening the railway companies, except the District and Tubes, had an improvised service.

The Prime Minister had an audience of the King yesterday. There was no indication last night of any attempt to resume negotiations between the Prime Minister and the T.U.C. The Prince of Wales returned to London from Biarritz last night travelling from Paris by air.

▲ *Though shortlived, the General Strike of 1926 was a harbinger of the social dislocation of the 1930s.*

▼ *During the Depression, Ramsay MacDonald was called upon to head a National Government.*

which seemed at the time to have no dynastic implications. The Prince of Wales, after all, would marry soon and produce a male heir to the throne.

The birth was of moderate, but far from all-consuming, interest to the newspapers. The baby was a relatively minor royal, and besides the country was more concerned with industrial unrest and the danger that it was heading for a General Strike. Postwar depression had set in, and the nation's miners were in a mood of militancy over the coal owners' threat to cut their wages.

The strike, when it came, lasted nine days; much of the country was shut down, with the notable exception of *The Times*, which managed to keep publishing despite a raid on its precious newsprint supplies by the Home Secretary, Winston Churchill, to publish his own propagandist British Gazette.

It was an early sign of economic recession which would get much worse before it got better. In 1931, in the wake of the Wall Street crash, for the first time the Bank of England was forced to print paper money unsupported by gold, and by 1933 unemployment had reached a peak of nearly 3 million. Ramsay MacDonald's National Government was forced to lay the first building blocks of the welfare state with the creation of the Unemployment Assistance Board. The century-old gospel of unbridled free trade had to be abandoned, to be replaced by import tariffs to protect domestic industries and a fad for state intervention and planning which created everything from the British Iron and Steel Federation to the Milk Marketing Board.

The hardest-hit areas of Tyneside, central Scotland and South Wales sent their hunger marchers to London. In Britain and abroad, recession fuelled both fascism and its perceived antidote, communism. But the deprivation was patchy; new industries created new jobs in the south-east of England and by 1930 there were one million motor cars on the roads of Britain. Economic hardship certainly had no noticeable effect on the British aristocracy, apart from the odd duchess who thought it jolly sport to drive a London bus during the General Strike. The Duchess of York was not the bus-driving type; besides, she had a newborn infant to look after.

Princess Elizabeth of York was only eight months old when her parents were obliged to undertake a six-month official tour of Australia and New Zealand, a major undertaking in the days before jet travel. They sailed on the battleship *Renown*, and returned with three tons of toys donated by a charmed Antipodean public for their greatly missed daughter, who could not quite pronounce her own name and called herself "Lilibet".

The birth of a daughter greatly altered the Yorks' lifestyle. In the early years of their marriage they had been the centre of a fashionable social whirl, familiar figures in the best London nightclubs where Elizabeth could indulge her passion for cocktails and dancing. Bertie enjoyed the cocktails, but was much less certain about the dancing.

The birth of a second daughter on 21 August 1930 further cemented family life. Princess Margaret Rose was born in a thunderstorm at Glamis Castle, making her the first member of the Royal Family to be born in Scotland since the future Charles II entered the world at Dunfermline in 1600.

In their first years of marriage the Yorks had lived at White Lodge, an inconvenient and run-down residence in Richmond Park. With a family in tow, they took over a spacious and vacant Crown Estate property at 145 Piccadilly. It was to be bombed in 1940; its site now occupied by the international hotels at Hyde Park Corner. It was a fine home, but lacked privacy; a curious public would crowd the upper decks of passing buses in the hope of catching a glimpse of the young princesses through the windows. As a private retreat, the King gave them Royal Lodge, a Regency villa in Windsor Great Park, where Elizabeth was able to indulge her passion for gardening by clearing and replanting its grounds. It remains a favoured weekend retreat.

As a patently close-knit family, the Yorks presented a sharp contrast to the glamorous but still-unmarried Prince of Wales, whose open dalliance with a succession of married women fed the gossip columns but offended society's more conservative elements. And he still showed no sign of producing an heir.

The full rosy, happy-family picture of the Yorks was not painted until 1950 when the princesses' former governess, Marion Crawford, finding herself a little hard up in retirement, published a book of memoirs. Miss Crawford, a formidable Scottish spinster, who trained as a teacher in Edinburgh, presented an almost entirely unblemished view of life with the Yorks: "No one ever had employers who interfered so little. I often had the feeling that the Duke and Duchess, most happy in their own married life, were not over-concerned with the higher education of their daughters. They wanted most for them a really happy childhood, with lots of pleasant memories stored up against the days that might come and, later, happy marriages."

But Crawfie had committed the unforgiveable sin of indiscretion. The Royal Family cut her dead, not sending so much as a wreath to her funeral, an indication of the unforgiving nature of her former employer. All royal staff now sign a confidentiality clause in their employment contracts.

Public perception of the Yorks as a popular family was bolstered

As a patently close-knit family, the Yorks presented a sharp contrast to the glamorous but still-unmarried Prince of Wales, whose open dalliance with a succession of married women fed the gossip columns but offended society's more conservative elements.

▼ *The 'black sheep', the Prince of Wales at point-to-point at Helmdon in Northamptonshire in 1921. Horse racing was among his more innocent pursuits.*

▲ *Fashions for Ascot, summer 1934.*
Whatever the economic and social
disruption of much of the 1930s, for some
life went on much as before.

▶▶ *Elizabeth with her first daughter, the*
future Queen Elizabeth II, May 1926.

by Bertie's greatly improved confidence in public, and by Elizabeth's refreshing charm as she went about the modest duties of a minor royal. Her informality, smile and pleasure in talking to all and sundry was a novelty, so unlike the rigidity of King George and Queen Mary. It impressed even *The Times*, which reported: "She lays a foundation stone as if she has just discovered a new and delightful way of spending an afternoon."

In 1935 King George V celebrated his silver jubilee, and professed himself amazed at the size and warmth of the crowd that lined his processional route to the service of thanksgiving in St Paul's Cathedral. The Yorks and their daughters played a prominent part in the accompanying festivities, winning their own generous share of public approbation.

But there were clouds in that sunny sky. In Germany, Chancellor Adolf Hitler ruled in the Reichstag of Berlin, figurehead of a growing movement of European fascism whose British arm had been founded by Sir Oswald Mosley in 1934. The spectre of rearmament was in the air.

The King himself was in poor health, being a heavy smoker in the days when medical opinion made no firm connection between his habit and his recurring bouts of bronchitis. The Prince of Wales was growing increasingly erratic in his behaviour and displaying little sense of princely responsibility.

He even had the effrontery to squire the principal interest in his life, the still-married Mrs Wallis Simpson, to the king's silver jubilee ball at Buckingham Palace. The lady from Baltimore was astute enough to detect unfriendly vibrations in the air, as she recorded many years later in her memoirs: "As David and I danced past the King and Queen, I thought I felt the King's eyes rest searchingly on me. Something in his look made me feel that all this graciousness and pageantry were but the glittering tip of an iceberg that extended down into unseen depths – depths filled with an icy menace for such as me."

Old King George was a bluff, gruff man of whom it was unkindly said that he did little but shoot defenceless birds and stick stamps in albums. But he was a wiser man than his critics would allow, and the clear favouritism he showed towards the Yorks and their family in his later years, and his increasing exasperation with his eldest son, indicated a fine perception of what the future might hold.

He died at Sandringham on 20 January 1936. In the last weeks of his life he confided to an old friend, Lady Algy Gordon-Lennox: "I pray to God that my eldest son will never marry and that nothing will come between Bertie and Lilibet and the throne."

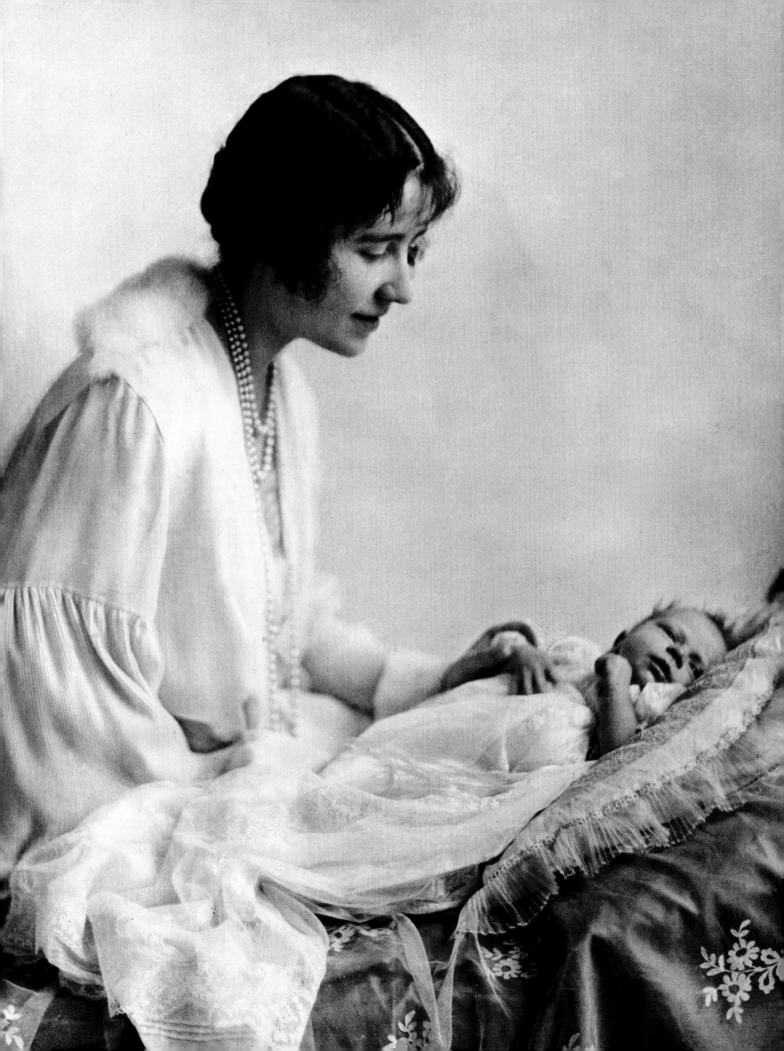

▼ ▶ *In 1927 the Duke and Duchess visited Australia and New Zealand. The year before, an Imperial Conference had set in motion the moves towards real independence for the Dominions, to be granted in 1931. The couple were forced to leave behind their eight-month-old daughter Elizabeth. 'It quite broke me up,' wrote the Duchess in a letter to her mother-in-law Queen Mary.*

▶ *The Duke and Duchess visiting Ashford in Kent in October 1926.*

 *Time off during the six-month tour of Australia and New Zealand. The Duchess of York lands an eight-pound rainbow trout (held by her bow-tied ghillie) at Lake Wanaka, South Island.*

▲ ▶ *Australia, again on the 1927 visit. The royal couple were present for Anzac Day on 25 April, honouring the Australian and New Zealand soldiers of the First World War, and for the state opening of the new parliament in Canberra, where they were greeted by a crowd of 50,000.*

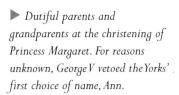 *On the wishes of her mother, the Yorks' second daughter, Margaret, was born at Glamis. The decision meant a long journey for Joseph Clynes, the Home Secretary of the day, who by an ancient law had to be present at every royal birth. This was the last such occasion that this curious custom was carried out.*

▶ *Dutiful parents and grandparents at the christening of Princess Margaret. For reasons unknown, George V vetoed the Yorks' first choice of name, Ann.*

▶▶ *The family with their newest member in a pram, at a garden party at Glamis in July 1931.*

◄ *Wimbledon 1926. The Duke of York and his partner, Louis Greig, being trounced 6-1, 6-3, 6-2 in the first round by the veterans A.W. Gore and H. Roper Barrett who, at 58 and 52, were over 20 years older than their opponents. The Duke and his partner were outclassed in front of an increasingly restive crowd. At one point, when the left-handed Duke had mishit several shots, a wag in the stand shouted, 'Try the other hand, Sir'.*

◄◄ *The Prince of Wales sporting a dapper beret. To the frustration of his enemies in the Establishment and within the Royal Family, the Prince was enormously popular with the public. He was a frequent visitor to factories, coal mines and working-class areas during the Depression, and conspicuously tightened his belt. Nevertheless he still found time for holidays. Here he is seen with his chum Prince Serge of Biarritz in August 1932.*

▶ *The Duke and Duchess of York back again at the Richmond Royal Horse Show in 1934. An eight-year-old Elizabeth pats the horse in the foreground.*

▲ *A visit in the summer of 1931 to a French colonial exhibition in Paris.*

▶ *Thanks to the King's recurring illnesses, and the Prince of Wales' growing waywardness, the Yorks shouldered more than their fair share of public duties. This picture shows the Duke and Duchess opening a new wing of Addenbrooke's Hospital in Cambridge in July 1932.*

■ The enthusiasm that greeted George V's silver jubilee on May 6 1935 seems to have genuinely moved the bluff and unbending monarch. The celebrations brought Londoners on to the streets in vast numbers, though the warm weather may have played its part, too.

On their return from the jubilee thanksgiving service at St Paul's Cathedral, the King and Queen stood on the balcony of Buckingham Palace. Looking down at the welcoming crowds with amazement, the King said, 'This is the greatest number of people I have ever seen in my life'. In the evening, the King addressed the nation on the wireless. Many of his listeners stood to attention while he spoke. (Top) The procession makes its way to St Paul's. (Above) The Yorks in the procession. (Above left) A street party in Battersea.

▶ *King George V died at Sandringham on 20 January 1936, his children dutifully gathered by his bedside. Some hours before the moment of death, the King's doctor had famously announced 'The life of the King is moving peacefully to its close.' In fact the doctor had resorted to euthanasia, allegedly injecting morphine and cocaine into the King's jugular. The picture shows the hushed and sombre multitude at a rain-swept Hyde Park Corner as the gun-carriage bearing King George's coffin turned into the Park.*

CHAPTER FIVE

ABDICATION AND ACCESSION 1936 – 1938

The Prince of Wales had decided as early as 1934 that he would marry Wallis Simpson, even though the slim, slightly harsh-looking lady from Baltimore was still wedded to her second husband, Ernest. By the time he ascended the throne as Edward VIII, Wallis had become the most significant person in his life.

THE NEW KING BECAME something of a recluse in his house at Fort Belvedere, near Windsor, sometimes displaying a cavalier disregard for his monarchical duties. Confidential state papers would lie around the house for any of his friends to read, and they would often be returned to the Government marked not only with the King's signature but with the telltale ring marks of carelessly abandoned cocktail glasses.

His erratic and irresponsible behaviour caused mounting concern to the Prime Minister, Stanley Baldwin, and to the Duke and Duchess of York. Bertie found the King increasingly unwilling to meet him, and relations between them grew ever more strained.

Until the death of George V, Elizabeth and Wallis Simpson had met only a handful of times and had exchanged no more than a few polite words. But when Elizabeth learned that the new King had dashed from his Accession Council – his first formal duty as monarch – to a secret assignation with Mrs Simpson at the Ritz, she was horrified at such seeming disregard for the dignity of high office.

Shortly afterwards the King took Mrs Simpson to visit the Yorks at their home at Royal Lodge, Windsor, and to show off a newly acquired American car to his brother. Years later Wallis recalled the meeting in her memoirs: "The Duchess of York's justly famous charm was highly evident. It was a pleasant hour, but I was left with the distinct impression that, while the Duke of York was sold on the American station wagon, the Duchess was not sold on David's other American interest."

Elizabeth's resentment was only just beginning, and had a long way to grow. When the King was invited to open a new wing of the Aberdeen Royal Infirmary, he declined on the dubious grounds that he was still officially in mourning for his father. He deputed Bertie and Elizabeth to do the honours. When Elizabeth subsequently discovered that, at the very moment of her plaque unveiling, the King had been seen in Aberdeen station waiting to meet Wallis off a train, both she and Bertie felt hugely betrayed. Not only was Elizabeth's strict moral sense offended, she could see the direction in which events were inexorably moving.

When it was learned that Mrs Simpson's divorce petition would be heard at Ipswich – chosen in preference to London in the hope that no one would take too much notice – on 27 October 1936, the signposts to the coming denouement were crystal-clear. Alec Hardinge, the King's private secretary, dashed to the Yorks' London home at 145 Piccadilly to warn them that they must prepare themselves to take over the throne. Bertie teetered on the edge of panic; Elizabeth remained calm, but was filled with a great sense of foreboding.

For the Yorks, the ensuing weeks assumed a nightmarish quality. Bertie tried in vain to extract from his brother his true intentions, but the King did his best to avoid both the issue and Bertie. When it became clear that the King faced the stark choice of woman or throne, his brother pleaded and begged him to stay.

But the brothers, once so close, were drifting apart, not least because of Elizabeth's ill-disguised hostility towards Wallis and to the entire notion of the King marrying her. At the height of the affair Elizabeth wrote to a friend: "The agony of it all has been beyond words, and the melancholy fact remains still at the present moment that he for whom we agonised is the one person it did not touch. Poor soul, a fearful awakening is awaiting his completely blinded reason before very long."

The King eventually told Bertie on 17 November of his intention to abdicate and marry. Later, as Duke of Windsor, David

It is unlikely that Elizabeth relished the prospect of her coming role, but any feeling of dread was balanced by a sense of challenge. She had ambition and confidence in herself; her worry was whether she could make enough of a man of Bertie.

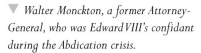

▼ *Walter Monckton, a former Attorney-General, who was Edward VIII's confidant during the Abdication crisis.*

recalled the meeting in his ghost-written autobiography: "Bertie was so taken aback by my news that in his shy way he could not bring himself to express his innermost feelings at the time." But Bertie could and did unburden his innermost feelings on his wife; they were feelings of the greatest distress, as were those of Elizabeth. A friend said of her: "She can forgive any act but treachery, but then she is as implacable as any Scot."

It is unlikely that Elizabeth entirely relished the prospect of her coming role, but any feeling of dread was balanced by a sense of challenge. She had confidence in herself, a confidence buoyed by a quiet and unspoken ambition for greatness; her worry was whether she could make enough of a man of Bertie.

In the Cabinet and other high places, discussion on the future of the throne reached a new earnestness. The King had his supporters, including Winston Churchill and the press barons Alfred Harmsworth and Lord Beaverbrook who, along with *The Times* and the rest of the British press, maintained a conspiracy of silence on the King's dilemma – in case, according to Geoffrey Dawson, editor of *The Times*, the King's judgement should be clouded by newspaper comment. True enough in Dawson's case, but the pro-marriage faction were not so much supporters of the King as political opponents of Prime Minister Baldwin. There was some talk of the formation of a King's Party, but it never took wing.

The King would have to go, and the only serious debate centred on who his successor should be. Some briefly favoured the King's other brothers, both of whom had male heirs. Gloucester was quickly ruled out as being incapable of the challenge and entirely uninterested in it. Kent was thought marginally more charismatic, but his private life was distinctly dubious. There was, in truth, no contest.

Baldwin and Cosmo Lang, Archbishop of Canterbury, had no doubt that it should be Bertie. He enjoyed indifferent health, was not overly bright, might well not be up to handling the coming crisis in Europe and had only daughters for heirs. But he had one overriding asset – a strong-minded, hugely popular wife, the darling of Scottish regiments and hospital wards alike, a woman of strong faith and high moral principles.

The deed was done on 11 December 1936. King Edward VIII, still uncrowned, signed his instrument of abdication and broadcast to the nation, speaking generously of his brother's fitness to succeed him: "He has one matchless blessing, enjoyed by many of you and not bestowed on me – a happy home with his wife and children." The hand of Churchill was behind those words.

▲ *Geoffrey Dawson, Editor of* The Times, *from 1912-19 & 1923-41*

▼ *Beaverbrook wrote of the Abdication, 'I am numbered amongst those who hoped for another solution.'*

▲ *The lives of the Yorks were increasingly overshadowed by the antics of Bertie's eldest brother. In August 1936, the new King Edward VIII took Mrs Simpson on an astonishingly indiscreet Adriatic cruise. The King, his married mistress on his arm, shamelessly paraded in front of the world's press. For the moment, Fleet Street did not breathe a word.*

▼ *The newspaper-reading public learn of the Abdication of the King on 11 December 1936. The Speaker of the House of Commons read out the Instrument of Abdication to a packed, solemn chamber. Baldwin rose in reply, saying, 'No more grave message has ever been received by Parliament.'*

Those events of 1936 are generally referred to as the Abdication Crisis. But there was no crisis; the King, in his going, acted with perfect constitutional propriety. There was never any real danger that the government of the day might fall, and the transition to a new monarch was enacted smoothly and correctly. The events might be better regarded, not as a crisis, but a mission to rescue the monarchy from an unhealthy dip in public esteem. Baldwin, announcing the abdication to the House of Commons, spelt it out. "While the feeling which the people have towards the Crown largely depends on the respect that has grown up in the last three generations for the monarchy, it might not take so long, in face of the kind of criticisms to which it was being exposed, to lose that power far more rapidly than it was built up, and once lost I doubt if anything could restore it."

A true crisis would have been far more likely had the King stayed, and it would have been of a far graver sort. It would be an unfair exaggeration to suggest that King Edward was a Nazi sympathiser, but he might well have remained an appeaser. He and Mrs Simpson visited Hitler, who saw the couple as potential allies in his grand strategy of making a peace deal with Britain in order to concentrate his offensive on his real enemy, Soviet Russia. The high command of the Third Reich was certainly disappointed at the King's going, regarding Baldwin's real motive – perhaps not entirely wrongly – as being to defeat the pro-German forces in Britain who they thought were working through the King and Mrs Simpson to persuade the British government into an Anglo-German entente. That was certainly the view of Hitler's ambassador in London. A Foreign Office paper drawn up at the time recorded a conversation between an FO official and a German diplomat: "Herr von Ribbentrop [the German ambassador] held this view strongly, more particularly as he had based the whole of his strategy on the role that Mrs Simpson was expected to play in Anglo-German affairs. Her disappearance had completely disconcerted him and he now views the future with considerable anxiety, since he feared that the new King would be content to follow the Foreign Office policy."

The paper further quoted the German diplomat, a Dr Jackh, as saying that "the Fuhrer himself was very distressed at the turn that affairs had taken in this country, since he had looked upon the late King as a man after his own heart who understood the Fuhrerprinzip and was ready to introduce it into this country." It was a compliment that would have caused even the late King to squirm.

Hitler may have been disappointed, but the new King was numb with shock. Pictures of Bertie leaving home to take his Oath of

Allegiance on 12 December show him pale, drawn and not entirely of this world. He knew he was replacing a king who, for all his weaknesses and lack of a wife, was the charismatic idol of millions. Bertie, on the other hand, had never even seen a state paper. Elizabeth remained his background strength. Shortly after the accession she wrote to Archbishop Lang: "The curious thing is that we are not afraid. I feel God has enabled me to face the situation calmly, and although I at least feel most inadequate, we have been sustained during these last terrible days by many, many good friends."

Taking the title of George VI to emphasise the continuity of the throne from his father, the new King was at first received coldly by a public still unused to such an apparently unglamorous monarch and unsure of his fitness for the role. But by the time of their coronation on 12 May 1937, the couple's popularity was assured.

Wallis Simpson was the *bête noire* of Elizabeth's life, and for the rest of her life she showed no sign of forgiving the Duke and Duchess of Windsor, although she did attend their respective funerals. Elizabeth's hand was undoubtedly behind her husband's blank refusal to grant Wallis the title Her Royal Highness, a matter which rankled with the Duke for the rest of his days. Yet Queen Elizabeth said many years later that she had never actually hated Mrs Simpson; she had just felt sorry for her. It did not always appear so.

A true crisis would have been far more likely had the King stayed, and it would have been of a far graver sort. It would be an unfair exaggeration to suggest that King Edward was a Nazi sympathiser, but he might well have remained an appeaser.

FROM THE PAGES OF THE  TIMES

December 14, 1936. The Accession of King George VI was proclaimed on Saturday in London and other capital cities of the Empire. His Majesty, being this day present in Council, was pleased to make the following Declaration:-

Your Royal Highnesses, My Lords and Gentlemen: I meet you to-day in circumstances which are without parallel in the history of our Country. Now that the duties of Sovereignty have fallen to Me I declare to you My adherence to the strict principles of constitutional government and My resolve to work before all else for the welfare of the British Commonwealth of Nations. With My Wife as helpmeet by My side, I take up the heavy task which lies before Me. In it I look for the support of all My Peoples. Furthermore, My first act on succeeding My Brother will be to confer on Him a Dukedom.

THE ARCHBISHOP'S BROADCAST
"STRANGE AND SAD"

The Archbishop of Canterbury, in his broadcast address last night, spoke of the absence of confusion, strife, and clash of

GEORGE VI PROCLAIMED
THE EMPIRE GREETS THE NEW REIGN
KING'S DECLARATION TO ACCESSION
COUNCIL BROADCAST BY THE PRIMATE

greater natural gifts for his kingship; yet, by his own will he surrendered his high and sacred trust because of a craving for private happiness. "Strange and sad," said Dr. Lang, "that for such a motive he should have disappointed hopes so high." He gave a sharp rebuke to King Edward's social circle, but he paid tribute to his long years of eager service to the Empire. The Archbishop referred feelingly to the universal sympathy with Queen Mary and to the gratitude due to the Prime Minister.

Turning from the past to the future, he spoke with hopefulness and confidence of the dawn of the new reign, and, as a personal friend for many years, paid tribute to the new King's personal qualities and the service he has already rendered to the State.

parties during the crisis as a wonderful proof of the strength and stability of the Throne and the steadiness of the people.

Referring to the ex-King, who "went out an exile," the Archbishop said that seldom, if ever, had any British Sovereign come to the Throne with

◄ *During the night of 11–12 December 1936 the ex-king arrived at Portsmouth to sail into exile on board a British destroyer.*

▼ *Edward and Mrs Simpson married in France on 3 June 1937. There was to be no forgiveness from his mother Queen Mary. She wrote to the* exiled Edward, *'It seemed inconceivable to those who made such sacrifices during the war, that you, as their King, refused a lesser sacrifice.'*

▶ *12 May 1937 had been the date set for the coronation of Edward VIII. All the usual souvenirs had been produced. But now, 14 years after their wedding there, it was Elizabeth and her husband who found themselves the focus of the ceremony in Westminster Abbey. Elizabeth wore a gown of ivory satin embroidered in gold thread with the emblems of the British Isles and the Dominions. In spite of some snags and fumbles the ceremony, broadcast around the world, was a triumph. The new King took the throne with a sense of guilt at what he saw to be his brother's gross dereliction of duty. 'I am new to the job,' he wrote to Baldwin soon afterwards. 'I hope that time will be allowed for me to make amends for what has happened.'*

◀ *The next day, the royal party drove in state to Windsor. After the drama of the Abdication, the public were not slow to transfer their affections to the new monarch and his consort.*

▶▶ *The family appear on the balcony of Buckingham Palace. The old Queen Mary is almost overcome, but Elizabeth and Margaret seem delighted with their mini-crowns.*

▲ *The King and Queen with Princess Elizabeth at the Coliseum for a performance in aid of the King George's Pension Fund for Actors and Actresses, 29 March 1937.*

◄ *At the opening of Coram's Fields and Harmsworth Memorial Playground, formerly the Foundling Hospital, in 1936.*

▲ *Queen Elizabeth, King George VI, Princess Elizabeth and Princess Margaret in the grounds of Holyroodhouse in July 1937, where the King inspected the Royal Company of Archers. With his wife's support the King's public appearances became increasingly assured. 'He's coming on magnificently,'*

Ramsay MacDonald told the Queen, rather patronisingly, as they both watched George VI speaking at a public function. 'And how am I doing?' she mischievously asked the former Prime Minister. 'Oh you...!' said MacDonald. Her fitness for the role had never been in doubt.

▶▶ *A study by photographer Marcus Adams from April 1940. The affection of mother and daughters for one another is touchingly clear.*

CHAPTER SIX

WORLD WAR II
1939 – 1945

The test of whether King George VI had the fibre to be the figurehead of a nation at war was not long in coming. But, in his brief apprenticeship he and Queen Elizabeth scored two notable triumphs.

THEY MADE TWO KEY overseas visits on which they had to sell both themselves and the notion that in the wake of the Abdication Britain remained a strong and stable democracy well braced, if not entirely prepared, for the trials to come. Subsequent events proved that in one case they had laid the groundwork of support and hope for a nation soon to fall to enemy occupation, and in the other they had helped smooth the path towards the American effort to liberate Western Europe.

For their state visit to France in 1938, the Queen asked a young and relatively unknown couturier, Norman Hartnell, to design a set of outfits that would enable her to hold her own in the world capital of high fashion. Taking *haute couture* to the French was a bold and

risky manouevre; Hartnell responded with a stunning array of white, and the Queen shimmered through her visit as though she had stepped from a Winterhalter painting. All Paris talked of *La Reine Blanche* for years afterwards, and Hartnell was created an Officier d'Academie.

The following year's visit to Canada and the United States, at the invitation of the Canadian Prime Minister, Mackenzie King, and President Roosevelt, had a far more serious purpose in bonding the two sides of the Atlantic for the European conflict that could not now be long postponed.

Accompanying the King to the opening of the Canadian federal supreme court building Queen Elizabeth, on the spur of the moment, invented the royal walkabout. It has

▲ *After a successful trip to Paris in 1938, the following year Elizabeth and her husband travelled across the Atlantic to drum up solidarity in case of war.*

▼ *Visiting an Indian encampment at Calgary, Alberta, May 1939.*

been one of her finest achievements in public relations.

She learnt that some of the stonemasons who had worked on the building were from her own native Scotland. Breaking all precedent and protocol, she peeled off from the official party, sought them out in the huge crowd, and spent a good ten minutes with them in couthy reminiscence of home. The crowd, astonished at what is now a commonplace, went wild at the sight of a royal prepared to jump the strict tramlines of ceremonial.

On the same tour, laying a wreath at the Ottawa war memorial, the Queen again broke away to find a group of war veterans, whom she felt were being left out of the action. It was a small gesture made the more dramatic by being unexpected, but the crowd of 70,000 left the Queen in no doubt that such informality would always be appreciated in the New World.

Lord Tweedsmuir, the Canadian governor-general (better known as the Scots novelist John Buchan) judged the royal tour a triumphant success. "The Queen has a perfect genius for the right kind of publicity," he wrote to a friend. "The unrehearsed episodes here in Ottawa were marvellous." The message of informality did not apparently precede the King and Queen to their next destination, Washington. Eleanor Roosevelt worked herself into a spin preparing the White House for her royal guests, only to discover that the King preferred a stiff drink to tea from bone china cups and that the Queen could not wait to change into a swimsuit and dive into the private pool.

Accompanying the King to North America on the eve of war was probably the most important and significant overseas visit that Queen Elizabeth ever made. Such was her popularity with the public that both Roosevelt and Mackenzie King must have found it somewhat easier to sell to their electorates the idea that the New World should come to the rescue of the Old Country when the time came.

During the twilight of peace in 1938, the King was undeniably on the side of the appeasers who wished to negotiate with Hitler rather than confront him. He was a staunch supporter of his Prime Minister, Neville Chamberlain, and greatly admired the efforts of an exhausted 70-year-old statesman making the first flight of his life to beard the Fuhrer in his Bavarian lair. Bertie, with his wife's support, even drafted a telegram to Hitler, pleading with him "as one serviceman to another" to avoid a repetition of the horrors of the Great War. He thought that such a direct approach might strengthen the hand of his government in its efforts to keep the peace. However, Lord Halifax, the Foreign Secretary, whilst acknowledging that a direct approach might be of some value, doubted the wisdom of the "serviceman" approach. He advised the King to wait.

Chamberlain thought that such a telegram might only serve to elicit a dusty reply from the unpredictable Chancellor of Germany, which would simply inflame the situation further. The telegram was never sent. But the King, truly horrified at the prospect of another war, was unstinting in his praise for his Prime Minister when Chamberlain returned from Munich with his historic piece of paper.

Worry over the international crisis prevented the King from accompanying his wife to the John Brown shipyard on the Clyde on 27 September 1938 to launch the largest liner in the world, the 83,000-ton *Queen Elizabeth*. She read a message from him urging the people "to place entire confidence in their leaders who, under God's providence, are striving their utmost to find a just and peaceful solution to the grave problems which confront them." Just under a year later, Britain declared war on Germany.

The war, when it came, was phoney at first, although Princesses Elizabeth and Margaret were moved from London to the safety of Windsor Castle as the country was gripped by the fear of air raids. The Queen refused point-blank a request from Neville Chamberlain that they be evacuated to Canada. "The princesses would never leave without me, and I could not leave without the King, and the King will never leave," she replied crisply. The decision was of incalculable value to national morale.

But special precautions had to be taken as a result. A dedicated unit of the Brigade of Guards was formed to mount a permanent watch on the princesses at Windsor Castle. The King had regular target practice with a .303 rifle, and the Queen with a .38 revolver, in the gardens of Buckingham Palace. "I will not go down like the others," she declared, referring to other European royalty who had fallen or fled the Nazi advance.

At the start of the war, the Queen decided that she had better make some effort to understand the mind of the enemy, so she read *Mein Kampf*. She then sent a copy of Hitler's autobiography to Lord Halifax with a note: "I do not advise you to read it through or you might go mad, and that would be a great pity. Even a skip through gives one an idea of his mentality, ignorance and obvious sincerity."

During 1940 the dominoes of Europe rapidly fell before the Nazi advance: first Norway and Denmark, then Belgium and the

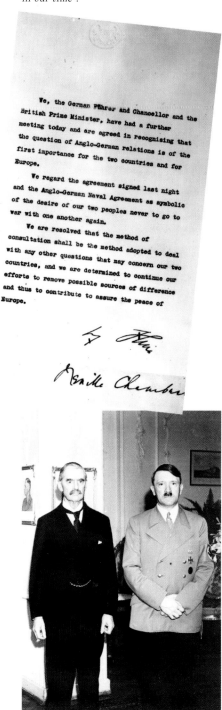

▼ The Munich Agreement of September 1938. Chamberlain hoped it meant 'Peace in our time'.

▲ Chamberlain, dogged to the last in his pursuit of peace, poses uneasily with Hitler during the Munich crisis.

In September 1938, the Queen launched what was then the world's biggest liner, the Queen Elizabeth. Even this happy event was overshadowed by the approaching conflict. The Queen read out a message from the King: 'He bids the people of this country to be of good cheer in spite of the dark clouds hanging over them.'

Netherlands and, worst of all, France, leading to the retreat of the British Expeditionary Force at Dunkirk. The news was all of defeat, relieved only by success in the Battle of Britain. Fought in glorious summer skies over southern England, it ensured that for the time being Hitler was deprived of air supremacy to cover an immediate invasion of Britain.

Defeat of the German fighter squadrons did not, however, deter their bombers. Hostilities hit the King and Queen with a vengeance on 12 September 1940, when a daring German pilot flew down The Mall and dropped a stick of six bombs on Buckingham Palace. The royal couple, who were in their offices at the time, were extremely fortunate not to suffer severe injury from flying glass and falling masonry. "A fine piece of bombing, if you'll pardon me, ma'am," said a Palace policeman to the Queen. "At least now I can look the East End in the face," she famously replied.

At the same time the King, replying to a note of condolence from the Cabinet, wrote: "Like so many of our people, we have now had a personal experience of German barbarity which only strengthens the resolution of all of us to fight through to final victory." Churchill noted in his diaries: "The King, as a sub-lieutenant in the Battle of Jutland, was exhilarated by all this, and pleased that he should be sharing the dangers of his subjects in the capital."

The East End bore the terrible brunt of incendiary and explosive bombing by an enemy intent on disabling the London docks. In November alone, 4,558 civilians were killed in air raids on Britain, and many thousands more rendered homeless. The King and Queen made regular visits to inspect the damage of the London docklands, and the Queen ordered her staff to rummage in the attics of the royal palaces to find spare furniture for the homeless. For the rest of her life, she remained a particular heroine to Londoners.

The King and Queen suffered with the people in other more domestic ways. Eleanor Roosevelt, on a visit in 1942 to glean information for her husband on the state of British morale, was surprised to find Bertie and Elizabeth enduring the same wartime privation as the rest of the country. She reported back how cold Buckingham Palace was for want of coal, how the King had a line painted round the inside of his bath to ensure no more than the regulation five inches of water, and how reconstituted dried egg and Woolton pie – an all-vegetable concoction devised to combat meat rationing and named after the then Minister of Food – were served on gold plates. With her Scots talent for thrift, the Queen in particular abhorred waste. On a visit to Lancashire at the height of the

Bomb damage in 1941 London. St Giles Church, Cripplegate is still standing in the background.

war, she found a gargantuan civic lunch laid on for her, which must have cost the town almost its entire quota of ration coupons for a month. She sharply rebuked the mayor: "We don't have any more food on the table at Buckingham Palace than is allowed to the ordinary householder according to the rations of the week." The mayor remained unabashed: "Ah well, tha'll be glad of a bit of a do like this, then."

In the early stages of the war the Queen had to accommodate and entertain various fleeing European leaders, including King Haakon of Norway, rescued by a British destroyer at Tromsø after being pursued the entire length of his country by the Nazi invaders, and Queen Wilhelmina of the Netherlands who arrived at the Palace gates with no personal possessions except a tin hat, her daughter Juliana and her granddaughter Beatrix.

▲ A ration book from November 1939. With shipping under attack from U-Boats, food supplies dwindled.

Another refugee given sanctuary by Britain was General de Gaulle who, when he left his exile to return triumphantly to Paris in 1944, told the King and Queen: "You are the only two people who have always shown me humanity and understanding." He was influenced, no doubt, by the Queen's excellent grasp of French.

Queen Elizabeth's real war work, however, was to act as partner, supporter and confidante to her husband. She was constantly by his side, and was often privy to the most confidential of audiences the King held with his own ministers and foreign ambassadors. As the prime minister of the day can offload his worries on his sovereign and be assured of absolute discretion and a fair dose of worldly wisdom, so the Queen was her husband's discreet sounding-board.

Yet she was acting as supporter to a man who was not in fact the most potent symbol of a nation at war, Head of State though he might be. To the British people, to the enemy and to the world at large, the personification of the war effort was unquestionably Winston Churchill. The Prime Minister did not set out to overshadow his monarch for whom he had the highest regard, but could hardly fail to do so.

Writing in *The Times*, the historian John Grigg argued: "Yet the monarchy was not eclipsed, because Queen Elizabeth was, in her very different way, a match for Churchill in the popular imagination. Her warm response to crowds and her sympathetic, cosy way of talking to individuals made her visits to blitzed streets and towns so memorable that they have passed into legend."

Elizabeth's strength was to convey a simple, homely patriotism, which she did at the King's side in all corners of the country. The royal couple's war work consisted largely of travel, and not only to the blitz-battered East End of London. They covered tens of

The King and Queen made regular visits to inspect the damage of the London docklands, and the Queen ordered her staff to rummage in the attics of the royal palaces to find spare furniture for the homeless. She abhorred waste.

▲ *George VI with the War Cabinet, August 1944. The King's relations with the War Cabinet improved steadily through the war, helped in no small measure by his regular and informal Tuesday lunches with Churchill. By the end of the war, the frostiness of George VI's and Churchill's early dealings had thawed dramatically. To the King's right is the Labour leader, Clement Attlee, deputy Prime Minister in the War Cabinet and Prime Minister from 1945. Whatever his regard for Attlee, George VI was nonetheless shocked at Churchill's defeat by Attlee in the July 1945 General Election.*

▼ *Wartime Britons were urged to collect scrap iron and steel for recycling into weapons.*

thousands of miles in the royal train, making low-key but highly morale-boosting visits to all parts of the kingdom, often arriving with little notice and saving money and disturbance to war-weary communities by sleeping on the train.

Herbert Morrison, the Home Secretary, became convinced that these visits did more to keep the people's spirits up than any other factor, particularly in the period up to late 1942. Until then, when the British Eighth Army chased Rommel's Panzer divisions out of North Africa, the Allies were suffering substantial losses of men and shipping. There was no significant victory to signal a turn of the tide in Allied favour and the Axis forces seemed impregnable to any attack, except that of a Russian winter at Stalingrad.

During those visits to the provinces, and indeed throughout the war, the King and Queen adopted a distinctive dress code. The King always wore uniform on public occasions, befitting the man in whose name the British armed services were fighting. The Queen never wore uniform, except for her regulation three strands of pearls. She was thereby able to personify the ordinary civilian, and especially the ordinary woman, left behind at home to suffer the trials of bombing, rationing and the worry over whether a husband, brother or son would return alive.

Queen Elizabeth added another particular role to her own war work: that of broadcaster. In 1941, she delivered a message of sympathy to the women of France, which made a profound impression on those in the occupied country who heard it.

In the same year, with Churchill's help with her script, she broadcast to the United States, expressing Britain's thanks for discreet American help being given. She wrote out a draft and sent it to Churchill with a note: "I fear it is not very polished – a good deal of my own. But I do want to thank the women of the US for their help and sympathy, and encourage them to further efforts." Churchill replied: "I may say I think it is exactly what is needed, and it is only with great hesitation that I have suggested a few alternatives."

The fortunes of war finally began to turn in earnest with the mounting of the greatest seaborne invasion in history to storm the Normandy beaches on D-Day, 6 June 1944. When the King learned of the plan, he desperately wanted to join the invasion force to see the action for himself. So, it transpired, did Churchill. The Queen encouraged her husband, knowing that he had spent the war in a state of frustration at not being a member of an active fighting force.

But Sir Alan Lascelles, his private secretary, recoiled from the proposal in horror, pointing out that no invasion commander could possibly mount a beach landing and ensure his monarch's safety at the same time. Besides, the King would not be able to see anything anyway. Sir Alan persuaded him not to go, and urged him to persuade his Prime Minister not to be so silly either. Neither man went on the day, but the King got his wish nine days later with a visit to invasion troops in France.

The King made many battlefront visits during the war, while Elizabeth struggled to maintain family life at home, often with difficulty. She and the King were separated from their daughters all day, and often for days at a time as they toured the country. But they were pleased to allow their elder daughter Lilibet into uniform when, on her 18th birthday, she was old enough to join the Auxiliary Territorial Service. The future queen plunged into an alien world of motor vehicle maintenance with her customary enthusiasm and seriousness. "We had sparking plugs all last evening at dinner," her mother told a friend.

As the tide of war turned decisively and the Allies began to repossess Europe from east and west, one nasty and far more domestic surprise lay in wait for the Queen, an incident experienced in mirror-image by her daughter nearly 40 years later.

Dressing for dinner in her bedroom at Windsor, the Queen was startled to see a man's hand emerge from behind a curtain and grab her by the ankle. "For a moment my heart stood absolutely still," she later recalled. The man meant no harm; he was an army deserter demented with grief at the loss of his entire family in an air raid who had got himself a job as a maintenance man at the castle and had entered the room on the pretext of changing a lightbulb. He only wanted to talk. "Tell me about it," said the Queen calmly while inching towards the bellpush to summon help.

When victory in Europe was declared on 8 May 1945 the celebrations were unbridled, although it was to take another three months and the dropping of two atomic bombs on Hiroshima and Nagasaki for the war in the Far East to reach its conclusion.

In London, before a crowd of hundreds of thousands, the Royal Family and Churchill took no fewer than eight curtain calls on the balcony of Buckingham Palace. It was, as one writer observed, the greatest victory celebration since Napoleon came back from Austerlitz. The cheers were for Churchill, but also for the man and woman standing beside him. In nine years the woman had transformed the man from an amiable nobody to a king of stature, a

▲ *A post-war atomic test. At Hiroshima and Nagasaki a new generation of terrifying weaponry had been born.*

When the King learned of the plan to storm the Normandy beaches, he desperately wanted to see the action for himself. The Queen encouraged her husband, knowing that he had spent the war in a state of frustration at not being a member of an active fighting force.

fit monarch for a dark hour.

The King went to Westminster to receive formal addresses from both Houses of Parliament on the conclusion of the war. The King, in reply, spoke highly of the efforts made by the fighting men of Britain and her allies, and by the civilian population. He then added: "I have done my best to discharge my royal duty as the constitutional sovereign of a free people, and in this task I have been unceasingly helped by the Queen, whose deep and active sympathy for all my subjects in pain or peril and whose intense resolve for victory has comforted my heart never more than in our darkest hours."

Those who, in the dying days of peace – the King, the Queen and *The Times* among them – supported a policy of appeasement, of allowing Nazi Germany to have Czechoslovakia if it would then lay off the rest of Europe, may be seen in hindsight as weak-willed and unwilling to confront reality. But they were of a generation that could recall all too vividly another European conflict that had ended only 20 years before.

When all hope of negotiation had gone, and the Chancellor of Germany was seen truly to be a madman, the patriotism and resolve of King George VI became iron and unflinching. Queen Elizabeth had done her work well.

▲ *At the victory parade in 1946, ex-Prime Minister Churchill sits with the man who replaced him, Labour leader Clement Attlee.*

▶▶ *Inspecting bomb damage at Buckingham Palace, September 1940.*

FROM THE PAGES OF **THE TIMES**

2½ YEARS OF FOOD RATIONING

APRIL 11, 1942. Food rationing was resumed after a break of 20 years on January 8, 1940, 18 weeks after the start of the war. The Times, in a leading article on November 2, 1939, had stated that it was "to begin gently," and the accuracy of that description will be even more apparent to-day than it was two and a half years ago, for when rationing came in again it covered at first only bacon, butter (allowing 4oz. with no check on purchases of margarine), and sugar (12oz. against 8oz. to-day).

It may be found useful to have printed together the amounts of the various rationed foods to which at present the individual citizen is entitled:– MAIN FOODS (WEEKLY) – MEAT: 1s. [5p] worth of butcher's meat: 2d [1p] worth of tinned corned beef or pork. Half this amount for children. BACON : 4oz. FATS : 8oz. (6oz. of butter and margarine, of which not more than 2oz. may be butter, and 2oz. of cooking fat). CHEESE:3oz. (12oz. for certain workers, including agricultural, forestry, and land drainage, the auxiliary force of the Women's Land Army, county roadmen, train crews, signalmen and permanent way men without access to canteens, miners, and vegetarians who do not take their meat or bacon rations). SUGAR : 8oz. TEA: 2oz. POINTS FOODS – Beginning with the four weeks period which

started on Monday each consumer is allowed 24 points. These may be expended as follows:– TINNED SALMON – Grades 1 and 11, 32 points a lb., or from 32 to 8 according to the size of the tin: grade 111, 24 points a lb, or 24 to 6 according to size of tin. SARDINES – From 3 to 36 points according to size of container, or 24 a lb. net. OTHER TINNED FISH – From 1 to 24 points a tin according to size or from 12 to 16 points a lb. TONGUES – 24 points a lb. MEAT ROLL OR GALANTINE – 21 points a 3lb. container or 8 points a lb. OTHER TINNED MEATS – 8 points a lb. RICE, SAGO AND TAPIOCA – 2 points a lb. BREAKFAST CEREALS – Containers of 8oz. and under, 2 points; up to 12oz., 3 points; over 12oz. 4 points. DRIED PEAS – 4 points a lb.

IMPORTED DRIED BEANS – 1 point a lb. SPLIT PEAS AND LENTILS – 2 points a lb. TINNED FRUIT – From 8 to 16 points a tin, or after removal from container 8 points a lb. TINNED PEAS – 3 or 4 points a tin. TINNED TOMATOES – 3 to 9 points. Eggs are not rationed in the official sense: they are allocated. The latest allocation provided for three a head in March. MILK – Expectant mothers and children up to six years, 1 pint daily; children and adolescents from six to 17, 1/2 pint daily; invalids up to 2 pints daily; other adults 3 pints weekly.

FEED ME WITH YOUR SCRAPS FROM
VEGETABLES & ANIMAL
MEAT BONES LARDER
POTATO APPLE PEEL

HE DOES NOT EAT *Rhubarb Tops, Tea Leaves, ...Green ...*
Skins of Banana Fruit, Oranges, Lemons & Bananas, or Salt, Citrus & Cocoa.

■ The trip to Canada and the United States in 1939 was a huge success for the Royals and the Queen in particular. From a party at the British Embassy in Washington a guest remembers, 'The Queen was superb. She was utterly unlike anything we had expected, queenly but human, regal but sympathetic.' Important friendships were also made with President Roosevelt and his wife, Eleanor. While they were abroad, the Duke of Windsor made an embarrassing broadcast from the Great War battlefield of Verdun which amounted to a call for peace at any price.

The Queen visiting the headquarters of the voluntary nursing and first aid services, on 6 September 1939, three days after war had been declared.

On 12 September 1939 Queen Elizabeth visited air-raid shelters at Bermondsey. On the day of the declaration of war, the air-raid sirens had sounded in London. It was a false alarm, but far worse was to come.

A visit to Aldershot to see a demonstration of the Mechanised Army in April 1938. In a speech a year later, the King praised the vigour of the rearmament being undertaken, 'Not to provoke war but to preserve peace.'Yet despite the King's fervent wish to avoid war, British rearmament was too little, too late. Even eight months after the declaration of war, British troops were powerless to halt the Nazi invasion of Europe.

■ *Visits to armaments factories by the King and Queen in the early days of the war were deemed vital morale boosters. (Right) an aircraft factory in Bristol receives a royal visit in February 1940; (below) a visit to an armaments factory in Birmingham in April the same year. No more* *than a month after this picture was taken, France had fallen and Britain stood alone. Factories such as these became the 'front line', turning out just enough machines to ensure that Britain could hold out.*

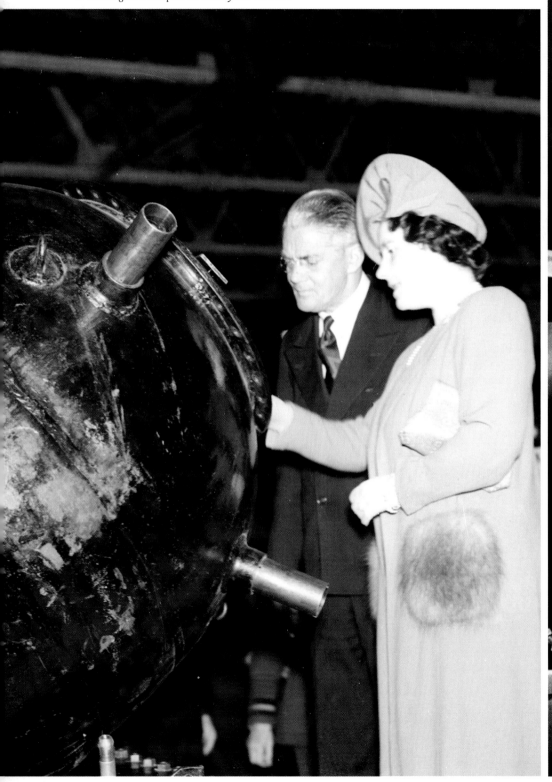

▲ The King and Queen visit Aldershot and inspect
a group of Canadian troops in 1941.

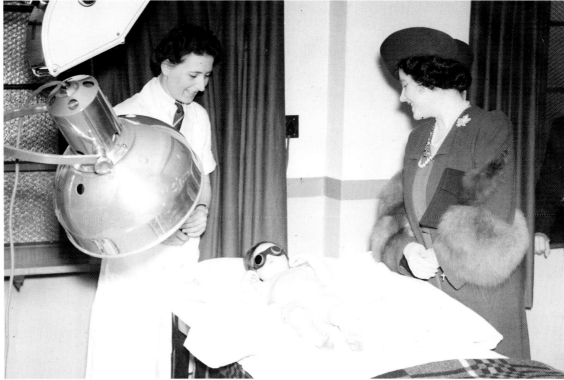

▲ At a Battersea day nursery for children in March 1942.

▼ At a bomb-damaged nursery in June 1944. Queen Elizabeth, like the King, did all she could to support the war effort, travelling thousands of miles on her visits to bomb sites. A US newspaper nicknamed her 'Minister for Morale'.

▲ Queen Elizabeth, King George VI, Princess Elizabeth and Princess Margaret in harvest fields at Sandringham, August 1943.

◄ In the same month, the family pose in the vegetable garden at Windsor. From the beginning of the war, all Britons were urged by the government to 'Dig for Victory', and small gardens sprang up all over the country in an effort to make good the losses of shipping in the Atlantic. In 1940 alone, a thousand ships were sunk by enemy action, a quarter of the British merchant fleet.

►► Visiting members of the Women's Land Army, Berkshire, July 1944.

▶ *A solemn wartime group at Buckingham Palace in February 1942 celebrate the christening of Prince William of Gloucester, here held by his mother, Princess Alice, Duchess of Gloucester. By this stage in the war, Queen Elizabeth had turned the Palace into an engine-room of the war effort, its grand halls the headquarters for her many working parties, mass-producing dressings and 'comforters' for British troops.*

▲ US troops fighting along the Caen-Falaise road in August 1944. A strong armoured thrust in the west of France, heavily supported from the air, punched a hole in the German lines and raced south and east. With Hitler refusing to countenance any retreat, the bulk of the German forces in France were encircled in the area around Falaise. In the ensuing panic, German military power in France was effectively ended.

▶ British troops check equipment having captured a German bunker at Cleve in western Germany in February 1945. Hitler's last counter-offensive in the west had failed and the Red Army was closing in from the east.

▲ The 'Big Three' Allied leaders meet at Yalta in the Crimea in February 1945 to discuss the final defeat of Nazism. Potential postwar tensions were already apparent.

◄ Crowds gather in Piccadilly to hear the news of victory in Europe.

▶▶ *On VE-Day the King, Queen and the two Princesses appeared on the balcony of Buckingham Palace and were called back out by the crowds no fewer than eight times. As Churchill noted, 'This war has drawn the throne and the people more closely together than ever before.'*

CHAPTER SEVEN

BEREAVEMENT: FROM QUEEN TO QUEEN MOTHER 1946 – 1953

At the end of the war King George VI was a man of only 50

who ought to have been in the prime of his life. But his

health, never robust, had been broken, partly by the strains

of war but more so from a lifetime as a heavy smoker.

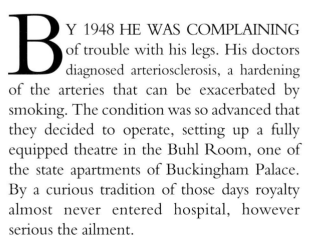

BY 1948 HE WAS COMPLAINING of trouble with his legs. His doctors diagnosed arteriosclerosis, a hardening of the arteries that can be exacerbated by smoking. The condition was so advanced that they decided to operate, setting up a fully equipped theatre in the Buhl Room, one of the state apartments of Buckingham Palace. By a curious tradition of those days royalty almost never entered hospital, however serious the ailment.

At one stage the doctors disclosed to Elizabeth that amputation of his leg might be necessary, as they feared the onset of gangrene, so poor had the blood circulation become. Such a drastic measure proved unnecessary, but the King's health continued to decline. In 1951 Elizabeth learned that her husband had cancer of the lung. Early the following year he waved off his elder daughter and her husband on a tour of East Africa. The picture of him on the tarmac is of a gaunt, exhausted and sick man; his daughter never saw him again.

He died in his sleep at Sandringham on 6 February 1952. At that moment his wife ceased to be Queen Consort and became Queen Dowager; his daughter, far away on safari in the Aberdare National Park of Kenya, remained blissfully unaware for some hours that she was now Queen Elizabeth II.

The King's death engendered the deepest grief in his widow and in the nation at large. That Elizabeth had done her work in guiding him to greatness was shown by the fact that the queue to file past his lying-in-state in Westminster Hall stretched at one stage for three miles.

On her accession his daughter said of him: "Much was asked of my father in personal sacrifice and endeavour, often in the face of illness. His courage in overcoming it endeared him to everybody. He shirked no task, however difficult, and to the end he never faltered in his duty."

His widow retreated into mourning at Birkhall, her house on the Balmoral estate, to contemplate her loss and her future at the age of only 51. She wrote to Edith Sitwell, who had tried to comfort her by sending a book of poems: "One thought how small and selfish is sorrow. But it bangs one about until one is senseless."

She was now in a position of no obvious purpose. She owed allegiance to her daughter, who had succeeded her father at the age of only 25. With old Queen Mary still alive, Elizabeth could not yet assume the role of family matriarch. Yet there was no doubt she had relished the position and trappings of Queen Consort; she was always a woman conscious of her position, and in her demure way keen that others should be conscious of it too. She was not the sort of woman to take Queen Victoria's approach to widowhood, shutting herself away for years on end.

Three months after the King's funeral, Elizabeth had a surprise visit at Birkhall from Winston Churchill, restored as Prime Minister after the Attlee interlude. What Churchill said is not recorded, but he seems to have persuaded her to resume something of a public life, and that she had a role to play. Doubtless, like Disraeli, Churchill laid on with a trowel the flattery to which she was always susceptible.

In 1947, the Royal Family travelled to South Africa. The visit was made at least partly to thank the South Africans for their wartime sacrifices in the struggle against Hitler.

Shortly after her conversation with Churchill, Elizabeth undertook the first public duty of her widowhood, reviewing the First Battalion, the Black Watch – her favourite regiment – as they embarked for the Korean War.

By the time of her daughter's Coronation in 1953, the stage was set for Elizabeth to assume the matriarchal role for which she was so patently well fitted. Queen Mary was dead, and Elizabeth was installed in her new official residence at Clarence House with her own small band of courtiers and staff under the direction of her new Head of Household, Group Captain Peter Townsend.

At the same time she bought a derelict castle at Barrogill on the extreme northern coast of Scotland, rebuilt it and renamed it Castle of Mey. It could serve as a retreat if required, but Elizabeth indicated that she had no intention of sinking into an early and vapid retirement. In a tribute to her late husband she had already said: "My only wish now is that I may be allowed to continue the work we sought to do together."

She adopted the title Queen Elizabeth the Queen Mother, which seemed to indicate a more positive approach to life than "Queen Dowager." A second career, far beyond the role of mere grandmother, was about to unfold.

The King's death engendered the deepest grief in his widow and in the nation at large. That Elizabeth had done her work in guiding him to greatness was shown by the fact that the queue to file past his lying-in-state in Westminster Hall stretched at one stage for three miles.

FROM THE PAGES OF THE TIMES

FEBRUARY 16, 1955. Plans for building 12 nuclear power stations during the next 10 years, at a cost of about £300m., were announced by the Government yesterday. It is hoped that building of the first two stations will start in

12 ATOMIC POWER STATIONS TO BE BUILT
£300m plan for next 10 years

1957, and that they will come into operation in about 1961.

The output of electricity from all 12 stations will equal the product of between five and six million tons of coal, and the cost of production at first will be about the same as at present. The intention is to supplement rather than to replace other forms of fuel such as coal.

The White Paper points out that new technical developments may lead to more rapid progress than has been forecast in the provisional programme; on the other hand, the programme may be too optimistic because the stations may take longer to build or cost more than has been estimated.

Nevertheless, the Government consider that those risks must be accepted, because "the development of nuclear power has reached a stage where it is vital that we should apply it commercially with all speed if we are to keep our position as a leading industrial nation and reap the benefits that it offers."

It was emphasized by Mr Geoffrey Lloyd, Minister of Fuel and Power, in the House of Commons yesterday, that

because of the nation's rapidly growing need for power, nuclear energy will supplement and not replace other forms of fuel; that coal mining will "remain one of the major employing industries of the country".

The demand for energy, particularly in the form of electric power, and increasing difficulty in producing the necessary quantities of coal, themselves would justify a great effort to build up a nuclear power system. The stations will be built by private industry for the electricity authorities, who will own and operate them.

The United Kingdom Atomic Energy Authority, as the only body with the necessary experience, will be responsible for giving technical advice on the nuclear plant. British industry and consulting engineers have as yet no comprehensive experience of nuclear technology. They face a major task in training staff, creating the necessary organization, and designing the stations.

The AEA, while giving as much assistance and advice to industry as possible, will remain primarily a research and development organization and will continue to design, build and operate pioneering types of power reactor, the "atomic furnace". They will also be responsible for buying uranium, processing the used fuel and extracting from it the by-product, plutonium.

The Royal Family's 1947 South African tour, with its long sea voyage there and back on HMS Vanguard, was seen as an ideal opportunity for George VI, still exhausted after the war, to recuperate. The journey itself was also one of the last times that parents and daughters would be together and away from the public gaze for such a relatively long time. Despite the slightly forced informality captured left, activities such as shooting competitions (below) helped ensure a relaxed mood on board. (Right) The King and Queen arrive in South Africa.

◀ ▼ *Perhaps inevitably, in the event the South African tour proved something of a long haul for George VI. In addition to the usual round of tiring public engagements, the hot, dusty weather was draining for the King. There were also political tensions. Many of the Boers had been incarcerated during the war for pro-German sympathies, and were in no mood to cheer those they saw as colonial overlords. One Boer host told the Queen that he could never forgive Britain for annexing his country. She promptly replied, 'I know. We feel much the same way in Scotland.' Group Captain Peter Townsend (main picture, front seat of car) accompanied the Royal Family on this tour.*

Princess Elizabeth had been unofficially engaged to Philip Mountbatten before the trip to South Africa, and when they returned *to Britain it was made official. They were married in Westminster Abbey on 20 November 1947. With rationing still very* *much in force, it was only by a special dispensation that the Princess was allowed 100 extra clothing coupons for her trousseau.*

The King and Queen at the wedding.

Queen Elizabeth arrives at Westminster Abbey for the wedding.

A scene from the Buckingham Palace balcony in April 1948 as the King and Queen celebrate their silver wedding anniversary. Left to right: Princess Elizabeth, the Duke of Gloucester, the Duchess of Gloucester, Queen Elizabeth, King George VI, Princess Margaret and Queen Mary.

The Jubilee thanksgiving service in St Paul's Cathedral. The Queen in a broadcast that evening spoke of 'our 25 years of happiness' and praised the institution of marriage.

Queen Elizabeth with the Royal Army Medical Corps for the Silver Wedding parade in April 1948.

The King and Queen attended a
performance of the musical South Pacific at
Drury Lane theatre on 30 January 1952.
Six days later, the King was dead.

▲ On 11 February, the King's remains were carried into Westminster Hall for the lying-in-state. Waiting at the entrance can be seen the veiled figures of the new Queen, Elizabeth II, Queen Elizabeth, the Queen Mother, the old Queen Mary and Princess Margaret.

▶▶ The funeral procession of George VI, up the nave of St George's Chapel, Windsor, led by the Earl Marshal and the Lord Chamberlain. Members of the Royal Family follow the coffin.

◀ The Queen Mother is welcomed at London airport on 13 May 1952 after a visit to Scotland. This is the first public photograph taken of her after the death of George VI. She wore black for a year. On the rare occasions she was persuaded to venture out, even make a speech, she would not risk her composure by mentioning her husband's name. When a friend told her what a brave face she was putting on things, she replied quietly, 'Not in private.'

▶▶ *The Coronation of Elizabeth II at Westminster Abbey on 2 June 1953. Some 8,000 people filled the Abbey, and for the first time, millions watched at home as the proceedings were televised.*

◀ *The golden state coach in Trafalgar Square on the way back to Buckingham Palace. Nearly three million people lined the streets to watch the brilliant procession.*

▼ *The official portrait at Buckingham Palace. Charles and Anne are in the foreground.*

The Queen Mother arrives at a ceremony to be made Honorary Freeman of the Grocers' Company in December 1953.

Elizabeth leaving Guildhall after receiving the freedom of the City of London in October 1953. Her wartime support for London had not been forgotten.

After the Coronation of Elizabeth II in 1952, the Queen Mother was anxious to allow her daughter the space to establish herself in her new role. Not that this meant an avoidance of royal duties for herself. Instead, she headed for a trip abroad. Here she is seen being entertained by dancers during her 1953 tour of Southern Rhodesia (now Zimbabwe).

During the 1953 trip, on which the Queen Mother was accompanied by Princess Margaret, the two Royals pay their respects at the grave of Cecil Rhodes, imperialist extraordinaire and founder of the two Rhodesias.

The Queen Mother sharing a joke with her daughter Queen Elizabeth II at the Badminton horse trials.

Walking the dogs at Sandringham in November 1956.

△ The Queen Mother and Princess Margaret arrive at the Coliseum Theatre for a production of Guys and Dolls in August 1953. Margaret here looks every bit the beauty who was by now taking London society by storm. But only two months earlier she had been forced to admit her relationship with the dashing but divorced Group Captain Peter Townsend.

As she emerged from her bereavement, Elizabeth, ever the royal trouper, gave no sign of her deep sense of loss.

A NEW LIFE
1953 – 1976

The year that saw the death of her mother-in-law and the crowning

of her elder daughter also sowed the seeds of a personal family crisis

for Elizabeth. During the coronation ceremony her younger daughter

Margaret had been seen by millions watching Britain's first major

television outside broadcast to flick a speck of fluff from the uniform

of Group Captain Townsend. It was the tiniest of signals but the whole

world knew in an instant that the 23-year-old younger sister of the

new Queen was in love with a divorced man.

BEFORE THE MONTH WAS out, Townsend found himself relieved of his post at Clarence House and assigned to a minor function at the British Embassy in Brussels. On the same day, Elizabeth flew to Rhodesia on an official visit that was intended to ease her back into public life. It being the dawn of jet travel, she flew on one of the revolutionary new breed of Comet airliners; more significantly, she took Margaret with her. Parting, it was felt, might cool the ardour.

It did not. Margaret and Townsend kept up a romance for nearly two years against an enormous weight of opposition from a deeply conservative Church of England and a self-righteous body of public opinion. Townsend, gracious to the last, said many years later that Elizabeth behaved impeccably throughout, exerting no pressure one way or the other on either party despite her own firmly held views on the sanctity of marriage.

Propelled by the church of which she is titular head, the new Queen was obliged to

With the birth of Prince Charles in November 1948, Elizabeth became a grandmother. Charles and Elizabeth developed an enduring bond. Here she accompanies him and Princess Margaret to Trooping the Colour in June 1951.

Again at Trooping the Colour, this time with Princess Anne as well as Charles, in June 1953.

remind her sister of the Royal Marriages Act, an 18th-century piece of legislation drawn up by George III in the hope of preventing his children making unsuitable liaisons. Until she reached her 25th birthday, Margaret would require her sister's permission to marry any man, divorced or not. Beyond that, both the Queen and the Queen Mother did their best to pretend that the romance was not happening, and declined to interfere.

Margaret's crucial birthday came and went in August 1955. Prime Minister Anthony Eden, himself divorced and remarried, flew to Balmoral to warn the Queen that several members of his Cabinet would resign if the marriage went ahead. Eventually, in October, Margaret and Townsend decided that the game was not worth the candle. After a long talk with her mother in the gardens of Royal Lodge, Margaret issued a statement announcing she had decided not to marry Townsend. Her mother said nothing, but must have been heartily grateful at the outcome.

As for Elizabeth herself, it was unlikely from the outset that she would ever sully the memory of her late husband by remarrying; indeed she never again showed the slightest romantic interest in any man. Instead she gathered round her a circle of rather effete male friends, of whom Noel Coward was *primus inter pares*: his light wit and love of the superficial appealed to her, coupled with the fact that he and his kind were never likely to argue with her, or engage her in uncomfortably controversial discussion.

Relieved of the burdens of state and the constant concern over her late husband's health, Elizabeth was able to give more attention to the role that, next to Queen Consort, was by far her most influential – that of grandmother. She saw much of her first, and always her favourite, grandson Charles; the two formed a strong bond which the Prince of Wales has acknowledged on many occasions since. One of the many things she taught him, for which he has been forever grateful, was a love of gardening. But, as a firm believer in the old cliché that work is the rent you pay for life, and equally drawn to public adoration, Elizabeth was unlikely to be content for long as a mere royal matriarch.

Her high-profile visit to America in 1939 had brought home to Elizabeth that she could command immense popularity as a public figure, and for the next 30 years she became an inveterate traveller, sometimes in an official capacity to other Commonwealth countries, most notably Canada, sometimes for her own unalloyed enjoyment. She made regular private visits to France, and particularly enjoyed Venice where, to her irritation, she was once photographed in a gondola and holding an ice-cream cone in the manner of a then-popular television commercial.

Some of her official overseas tours were on a heroic scale. In 1958 she embarked on a 30,000-mile, three-month odyssey around the world, visiting Canada, Honolulu, Fiji, New Zealand and Australia including Tasmania, an early indication of the revolution of jet travel which subsequently made Elizabeth's daughter the most widely travelled monarch of any nation in history. The Queen Mother circled the globe again in 1966, a trip postponed from 1964 to allow her to have her appendix removed. Between times she flew to Rhodesia (now Zimbabwe) and Zambia to open the mighty Kariba Dam on the Zambesi, where she was presented with six emeralds from a local mine and cheered along her route by a crowd of 60,000.

The African continent was a much-favoured official stamping ground for Elizabeth. Born when one-quarter of the world was still coloured pink on the map, she seemed to relish that old imperial conceit of a great white queen coming to bestow civilisation on the ignorant. As one colony after another broke the bonds of British rule, her travels in that part of the world gradually diminished although she continued to identify herself with, and sympathise with, Africa's white minority rulers to the last. There was no doubt whose side she was on when the rebel Ian Smith, Prime Minister of Rhodesia, declared illegal independence in 1965 to fend off British pressure for black majority rule in one of its last remaining African possessions. But there was still the trusty Old Commonwealth of Canada, Australia and New Zealand ready to welcome a distinguished emissary from the old country.

At home, Elizabeth shouldered her share of the workaday royal round, opening hospitals, touring factories, shaking the hand of countless worthies, always with the knack of never appearing bored and the talent for making the person she was talking to feel they had her undivided attention and interest.

She took on more than 300 patronages, most of them in keeping with her sense of propriety and decorum. Not for her the close human, physical contact with the terminally ill and the dying at which Diana, Princess of Wales, so excelled. She was far more at home as Colonel-in-Chief of the Black Watch, or in what were perhaps her two favourite honorary roles, Chancellor of London University and Lord Warden of the Cinque Ports, of which latter she was the first woman holder in the 900-year history of a post which originated as guardian of England's five key medieval Channel harbours.

Royal duties aside, the widowed Elizabeth happened upon another interest which rapidly grew into a consuming passion and

Relieved of the burdens of state and the constant concern over her late husband's health, Elizabeth was able to give more attention to the role that, next to Queen Consort, was by far her most influential — that of grandmother.

The Queen, Prince Charles, the Queen Mother and Princess Anne at the Badminton horse trials, April 1960. Royal life — particularly if there were horses about — could be surprisingly informal.

has remained so. At a dinner given by the King and Queen at Windsor in 1949, one of the guests had been Anthony Mildmay, five times champion amateur steeplechase jockey. She had always taken an interest in flat racing, but Mildmay convinced her that there were far greater thrills, for both owner and rider, over the jumps. Within weeks she had bought her first steeplechaser, Monaveen, for £1,000.

Elizabeth quickly learned the peaks and troughs of racehorse owning. Monaveen gave her four wins until he broke a leg and had to be destroyed. She was not deterred and ordered her trainer, Peter Cazalet, to build up her string, including a highly promising jumper named Devon Loch, which gave its royal owner six wins and her most celebrated disappointment. With Dick Francis in the saddle, Devon Loch was romping home to win the 1956 Grand National in front of a huge crowd, his owner and her daughters all hoarse with cheering, when, inexplicably and dramatically, he collapsed on the long final run-in.

Francis flung down his whip and wept. The fatalistic owner consoled him: "That's racing, I suppose," the Queen Mother told him, later presenting him with a silver cigarette box engraved "Devon Loch's National." The Queen Mother subsequently enjoyed a hugely successful career as an owner, with more than 500 winners, and Dick Francis went on to become an enormously successful popular novelist.

Elizabeth became a greatly admired figure in the racing world, not least because of her expert eye for a promising horse. She bought Then The Rip from a Norfolk publican for 400 guineas, and was rewarded with 13 wins, although her most successful purchase of all was Game Spirit, which gave her no fewer than 21 wins.

At one time in the 1960s Elizabeth had 19 horses in training, but so ruinously expensive is the career of racehorse owner that even she had to cut back in her later years. Yet in her late nineties she is still picking up the occasional winner's trophy – none more welcome than that delivered to her bedside as she recovered from her second hip operation at the age of 97 – and neither age nor weather deter her from regular appearances in the paddock. The family life which proceeded around her was less well endowed with winners. In 1960 her daughter Margaret married the commoner Antony Armstrong-Jones, and for a time the couple were the jewels in London's smart young social set. Within the space of four years in the early 1960s, Elizabeth was presented with four more grandchildren to add to Prince Charles and Princess Anne: Viscount Linley and Lady Sarah Armstrong-Jones from Margaret, and Prince Andrew and

▲ *Attending a race meeting at Folkestone in 1964. The Queen Mother bought her first steeplechaser, Monaveen, for £1,000 in 1949. Horse racing rapidly became a consuming passion.*

▼ *Prince Charles and the Queen Mother at the service commemorating the 900th anniversary of Westminster Abbey, 28 December 1965.*

Prince Edward from the Queen. In 1973 she attended the first wedding of a grandchild when Princess Anne married Captain Mark Phillips at Westminster Abbey. As the younger generation expanded, so Elizabeth's own generation began to fade away. In 1961 she lost, at the age of only 59, her younger brother David, to whom she had been so close in childhood. And in 1967 her elder sister Rose, the last surviving sibling, died leaving Elizabeth the sole surviving Bowes Lyon of her generation.

Castle of Mey, with its wonderful garden became an ever more important retreat for her. Hidden in a girdle of woodland to shelter it from the constant wind of the Pentland Firth, it is a child's drawing of a castle, its roofline all turrets and battlements. But it is homely, and on its 25 acres Elizabeth bred a prizewinning herd of Aberdeen-Angus cattle. She became an accomplished fisherwoman, standing waist-high in the icy waters of the Thurso River near Castle of Mey, and landing the biggest catch of her life – a 26-pound salmon – on the Dee at Birkhall on the edge of the Balmoral estate.

Elizabeth successfully established a profusion of her favourite rose, "dear old Albertine, ready to stand anything." Castle of Mey was the ultimate retreat where she could raise the drawbridge on the world. It was, in a way, a reflection of herself, a solid yet friendly little fortress in a harsh landscape, within whose stout stone walls the love and dedication of a skilled gardener conjured beauty from unpromising ground.

She became a greatly admired figure in the racing world, not least because of her expert eye for a promising horse. She bought Then The Rip from a Norfolk publican for 400 guineas, and was rewarded with 13 wins, although her most successful purchase of all was Game Spirit, which gave her no fewer than 21 wins.

FROM THE PAGES OF **THE**  **TIMES**

NOVEMBER 29, 1968. John Winston Lennon, aged 28, of The Beatles, was fined £150 with 20 guineas costs at Marylebone Magistrates' Court yesterday when he pleaded Guilty to the unauthorised possession of 219 grains of cannabis resin found when detectives accompanied by dogs searched his flat at Montagu Square, Marylebone on October 18.

Appearing with him on remand, Mrs Yoko Ono Cox, aged 34, artist, of the same address, denied charges of unauthorised possession of the drug and wilfully obstructing Detective Sergeant Norman Pilcher when he was exercising his powers under the Dangerous Drugs Act.

Mrs Cox was discharged and Mr Lennon was also discharged on a similar charge of obstructing the officer, which he denied. The prosecution offered no evidence on those three counts.

JOHN LENNON FINED £150 ON DRUG CHARGE

Mr Roger Frisby, for the prosecution, told Mr John Phipps, the magistrate, that although the flat appeared to be in the joint occupation of the couple, Mr Lennon had taken full responsibility for the drugs and said Mrs Cox had nothing to do with it. Mr Frisby said that when the officers got into the flat and told Mr Lennon that they had a search warrant they found a large quantity of drugs properly prescribed by Mr Lennon's doctor.

When asked if he had any he should not have, such as cannabis, Mr Lennon shook his head. Mr Frisby said a cigarette rolling machine found on top of a bathroom mirror, a tin originally containing film found in a bedroom and a cigarette case all bore traces of cannabis resin.

In an envelope in a suitcase was found 27.3 grains of the drug, and 191.8 grains was in a binocular case, nosed out by a dog, on the mantleshelf in the living room.

From the late 1950s, the Queen Mother developed a pronounced taste for overseas travel. Tours such as that in 1958 to Canada, the Pacific and then to Australia and New Zealand allowed her to indulge it to the full. Here she is seen in New Zealand.

Back in Rhodesia again in 1960, the Queen Mother is greeted by Chiefs Mukuni, Muskotwane and Sekute on her arrival at Livingstone

Looking out over the Vipya Hills and the Nyika plateau during the 1960 tour of Rhodesia.

Conferring degrees at the University of London.

The Queen Mother and Princess Margaret attending a performance of Noel Coward's Suite in Three Keys *in June 1966.*

The Queen Mother at the Caledonian Ball in May 1959 giving a spirited performance of the 'Dashing White Sergeant'.

The Queen Mother with Prince Andrew at Clarence House on her 60th birthday.

Laying the foundation stone for the new building of the British Insurance Association, in May 1961.

The Queen Mother with Princess Margaret, Lord Snowdon (Antony Armstrong-Jones) and their newborn son, David Linley, returning home from hospital, 30 November 1961. Princess Margaret and her husband epitomised a new kind of royal chic in the early 1960s. It was to prove only too transient, however.

The Queen Mother fixes a sprig of shamrock to the collar of Fiona, the Irish wolfhound mascot of the Irish Guards during the St Patrick's Day parade at Windsor in 1969.

The launching of the new liner Windsor Castle in June 1969.

A gun-carriage carries the body of Winston Churchill from Ludgate Hill to St Paul's. Of all the politicians they worked with, the Royal Family held Churchill in the most affection — almost as much for his sense of fun and mischief as for his indomitable wartime leadership.

On 14 November 1973 Princess Anne married Captain Mark Phillips. Though no royal rebels, Anne and Mark were nonetheless typical of their period in rejecting elements of the rigid public formality of earlier generations of royalty: there is nothing forced about the laughter in this picture. But the contrast went deeper than a readiness to let their hair down in public. The imperatives of royal duty, above all the absolute sanctity of marriage which the Queen Mother so fervently espoused, were also casualties of this more human face. Princess Anne's marriage ended in divorce, as did Princess Margaret's, Prince Charles's and Prince Andrew's.

CHAPTER NINE

GREAT GRANDMOTHER FROM 1977

The year 1977 was a significant milestone in the life of the Queen Mother. Already six times a grandmother, on 15 November she became a great-grandmother, further bolstering her position as the grand matriarch of the Royal Family.

PETER PHILLIPS, THE FIRST child of Princess Anne and Captain Mark Phillips, besides being Elizabeth's first great-grandchild, was a ground-breaker in at least two other ways. He was the first child so close to the throne to be born in hospital; his intensely practical mother did not hesitate to waive the tradition of royal births at home, and opted for delivery in the private Lindo wing of St Mary's Hospital, Paddington, under the supervision of George Pinker, the Queen's gynaecologist.

The child, fifth in line of succession at the time of his birth, was also the first in his position for nearly 500 years to be born without a title. His parents made a conscious decision at the time of their marriage that as far as possible they would keep the trappings of royalty at arm's length, and that their children would be raised somewhere close to the world of normality. It was, in its own way, a bold and radical decision, and one which widened yet further the gap between the modern Royal Family and the Victorian

Bunting in north London in celebration of the Queen's silver jubilee in June 1977. Like her grandfather George V in 1935, Elizabeth II was surprised at the public's enthusiastic response to the anniversary.

The beacon on Snow Hill at Windsor, lit to mark the beginning of the 1977 jubilee celebrations.

roots of Elizabeth's generation.

The year of Peter Phillips' birth was a year of good fortune for the Royal Family, with the Queen's silver jubilee celebrations turning out to be an unexpectedly popular success. The Labour Government of the day, embroiled in industrial unrest and economic gloom, wanted to ignore the event. Robert Lacey, an author who thought the Queen a suitable subject for a serious and analytical biography, hawked his manuscript round a succession of publishers, all of whom thought the idea of such scant public interest that it could not possibly sell. Princess Margaret's separation from Lord Snowdon had cast its own pall over royalty's public image.

But, in the event, the nation had a ball, with street parties reminiscent of those that celebrated the outbreak of peace in 1945. The Queen was lauded by her subjects who appreciated her 25 years of devoted service. Her mother basked in the reflected glory, recalling at first hand the similar unexpected adulation that had greeted King George V on his jubilee in 1935.

The jubilee seemed to give the lie to years of relative indifference by the public towards the Royal Family, and a regular background of open criticism which had begun as early as 1957 with the historian – and strong monarchist – John Grigg (then Lord Altrincham) who was threatened with a horsewhipping, and physically assaulted as he left a television studio, for criticising the Queen in a long and serious article on "The Monarchy Today". The criticism was constructive in intent but touched a raw nerve in those immediate post-coronation years. One criticism was that "the Queen, like her mother, appears to be unable to string even a few sentences together without a written text." This was particularly unusual in including the Queen Mother in a suggestion that the royals were not perfect. Attacks on the Royal Family, either as individuals or as an institution, have almost always spared Elizabeth, whether on the grounds of revered age, a distinguished war record or the fact that her almost total lack of public utterances deprives critics of any ammunition.

For many years the most consistent scourge of the entire apparatus of monarchy, on the grounds that it was a useless waste of a great deal of money, was the backbench Labour MP William Hamilton. But even Hamilton felt obliged to pay a most uncharacteristic tribute on Elizabeth's 80th birthday: "My hatchet is buried, my venom dissipated. I am glad to salute a remarkable old lady. Long may she live to be the pride of her family. And may God understand and forgive me if I have been ensnared and corrupted, if only briefly, by this superb royal trouper."

Elizabeth often appears to be the Royal Family's one firm

foundation, supporting them through recurrent domestic upheaval. She witnessed marital failure in one daughter and three grandchildren but, from her lofty High Victorian viewpoint, where serious courting meant holding hands in a boat, she was largely powerless to prevent any of it.

Her attitude to marriage is old-fashioned and strictly Christian, and although an outsider herself – albeit a high-born one – she is suspicious of those who enter the Royal Family without the pedigree of her own rigid standards of morality and commitment, which had enabled her to adapt to the bizarre and unreal lifestyle of royalty with the greatest success. In the cases of Mark Phillips, Lord Snowdon and Sarah Ferguson, her wariness could be said in hindsight to have been justified. But she seemed heartily to approve – in the beginning at least – of Lady Diana Spencer.

Diana was the granddaughter of one of Elizabeth's oldest and closest friends, Ruth, Lady Fermoy, who also served her for 37 years as a lady-in-waiting. Ruth had married Lord Fermoy who, because his peerage was Irish, was able to sit for some years as the Conservative MP for Norfolk. Ruth Fermoy's daughter Frances had married Johnnie Althorp, heir to the earldom of Spencer; their daughter Diana was therefore sprung from the very same stratum of aristocracy as Elizabeth herself. The difference was that Diana, unlike Elizabeth, was the product of a bitterly broken home. It was a rare event when Lady Fermoy entered the witness box of the divorce court to testify that her own daughter was not fit to be given custody of her children.

It would be an exaggeration to suggest that those two elderly and formidable grand-dames, Elizabeth and Lady Fermoy, sat over gins and plotted the marriage of their respective grandchildren. It would have been unnecessary: Diana was already perfectly well known to the Royal Family through her own family connections and the fact that her brother-in-law Sir Robert Fellowes was private secretary to the Queen. But at the same time, neither woman did anything to discourage the union.

Elizabeth's influence on the matter was nevertheless enormous. The Prince of Wales had two confidants from whom he sought advice and with whom he shared thoughts, his grandmother and his great-uncle Earl Mountbatten of Burma. Mountbatten was fiercely ambitious for his own bloodline to ascend the throne and hoped that Charles might marry his own granddaughter, Amanda Knatchbull.

She witnessed marital failure in one daughter and three grandchildren but, from her lofty High Victorian viewpoint, where serious courting meant holding hands in a boat, she was largely powerless to prevent any of it.

▼ *Diana, like the Queen Mother, established an immediate rapport with the public. But the differences between the two were as significant as their similarities. Diana's self-conscious glamour and New Age yearnings were in stark contrast to the Queen Mother's rectitude and sense of duty.*

▲ ▼ *The traditional photocall for the Queen Mother's birthday, August 1992. Four months later, Diana and Prince Charles separated. In the same month, Princess Anne was remarried, to Commander Timothy Laurence (below), at a modest service at Crathie Kirk, Balmoral.*

The Queen Mother, in common with some other members of the Royal Family, did not always wholeheartedly approve of Mountbatten's influence over the heir to the throne. Their objections were suddenly and tragically ended in 1979 when Mountbatten, together with three other members of his party, on his regular summer holiday in the west of Ireland, died at the hands of an IRA terrorist bomber.

That left Elizabeth the sole repository of her grandson's innermost secrets among his own family. The prince frequently and publicly praised her to the skies: "Ever since I remember, my grandmother has been the most wonderful example of fun, laughter, warmth, infinite security and, above all else, exquisite taste in so many things." Given such a close bond of intimacy and trust, it is extremely unlikely that Charles would have entered into the marriage without his grandmother's approval.

Elizabeth had high hopes for Diana, assuming that she would wear the mantle of royalty as effortlessly as she herself had done in 1923. But her hopes were dashed when what was initially portrayed as a love-match was eventually exposed as a marriage of convenience. Where Diana, controversial and flawed though she may have been, in some ways represented the future, Elizabeth stands for high and immutable values, but she nonetheless represents the past.

When the Waleses' marriage began to crumble, there was no doubt on which side Elizabeth's sympathies lay although, as ever, there was no public signal of the direction of her loyalties. She has been close to Charles since he was a baby, and that bond continued through her favourite grandson's marital collapse.

Relations between Diana and the Queen Mother soured. When the Princess unburdened herself to the author Andrew Morton, she let it be known that she saw Clarence House as the fount of all negative comment about herself and her mother Frances Shand Kydd. Diana believed that Elizabeth, bosom friend of Lady Fermoy, had become unfavourably disposed towards herself and her mother, and that she exercised a greater influence over her grandson than was healthy for a marriage. She kept what she called "a distrustful distance" from the Queen Mother, finding any social occasion hosted by her stiff and overly formal. The age, generation and attitude gap between the two women was, and remained, unbridgeable.

Differences in attitude were equally marked with Sarah Ferguson, who acquired the same title of Duchess of York that had been bestowed on Elizabeth at the time of her marriage. The well-publicised extra-marital antics of the second Duchess as her marriage collapsed were anathema to her predecessor, who throughout her life has displayed a positive hatred of any behaviour that might be classed as vulgar.

Elizabeth faced a dilemma following the third divorce in the series, that of her granddaughter Anne from Mark Phillips. The divorce was conducted cleanly and with no public rancour. Anne, who by now had accepted the title Princess Royal from her mother in recognition of her Stakhanovite appetite for hard work, wished to remarry, but felt she could not do so in an Anglican church which still officially frowned on second marriages. The solution was to marry Tim Laurence in the Church of Scotland, which had fewer reservations over blessing second unions.

Elizabeth debated for weeks over whether to attend, and up to the very last minute it was uncertain whether she would be present at the service, conducted on a bitterly cold December day in 1992 at Crathie Kirk by the gates of Balmoral. In the event she turned up, smiling at all and sundry as ever, but giving no clue to her true feelings, which can only have been mixed.

It had been the year that the Queen herself described at its end as her "annus horribilis" – divorce for the Princess Royal, separation for the Waleses, a disastrous fire at Windsor Castle and the first income tax demand to a reigning monarch since 1937. Faced with a rising call for the monarchy to deliver better value for money, the Queen relieved the taxpayer of the burden of paying the working expenses of her extended family. The only people subsequently funded by the state were herself, her husband and her mother. t is significant that of those politicians who demanded a reduction in the size of the Royal Family not one questioned the right of Elizabeth to her generous allowance from the public purse.

Elizabeth's secret, as ever, was to display that faultless public charm which even the queens of Hollywood would have found hard to sustain. During her octogenarian decade she reduced her public commitments, but not by much, still managing an annual foreign visit, supporting the Queen at state ceremonials and always inviting to tea any visiting head of state passing through London. Half an hour in the late afternoon at Clarence House became built in to the standard programme for all incoming state visits, from the President of France to the Emperor of Japan.

As she aged, she began to concentrate her public activities rather

When the Waleses' marriage began to crumble, there was no doubt where Elizabeth's sympathies lay. She has been close to Charles since he was a baby, and that bond continued through her favourite grandson's marital collapse.

▼ *The Duke and Duchess of York with Princesses Beatrice and Eugenie at a charity golf match, July 1998. The strain of divorce is banished for the camera.*

more on her favourite interests, notably her regiments. In 1983, only four years after the murder of Mountbatten and despite threats against her from the IRA, she flew to Northern Ireland to take the salute at the 25th anniversary parade of the Territorial Army at Ballymena. Security chiefs were terrified when, true to form, she wandered over to chat to the crowd after planting a tree at Hillsborough Castle, the seat of British power in Belfast.

But Elizabeth was not concerned with the risks inherent in making public appearances, only in the opportunities they afforded to meet her public. The Queen has always been wary of helicopters, using them only when there is absolutely no alternative. Her mother, on the other hand, saw their possibilities and took to their convenience with unabashed enthusiasm. "The chopper has changed my life as decisively as that of Anne Boleyn," she once remarked.

Her last major overseas visit was to Canada in 1989, when despite being within sight of her tenth decade she undertook a strenuous tour revisiting many of the places she had seen with her husband during their epoch-making visit 50 years before. And she visited Berlin to present shamrocks to the Irish Guards on St Patrick's Day, as the Wall was coming down and the division of Europe was ending. She had been 17 at the time of the Bolshevik Revolution; she was still alive to witness the end of the Soviet Empire 72 years later.

Her calendar retains its fixed points, including her annual visit to the Field of Remembrance at Westminster Abbey, where the lawn is planted with thousands of crosses in memory of the war dead; her regular appearance on a balcony to watch the Remembrance Sunday ceremony at the Cenotaph; and her annual tour of the Smithfield show, a showcase for British stockbreeding at which Elizabeth can converse knowledgeably, being a successful Aberdeen-Angus breeder herself. But the highlight of her public year is undoubtedly her birthday.

The tradition began informally, with a small crowd gathering outside Clarence House, enticing her out to sing Happy Birthday to her and present her with flowers, cards and the occasional cake. As each year passes the crowd grows bigger.

She relished the attention, and would regularly spend a good 45 minutes performing her walkabout, accepting gifts and exchanging pleasantries. When an increasingly troublesome arthritic hip made walking difficult, her staff hit upon the brilliant notion of a battery-powered golf buggy, driven by her regular chauffeur, which enables her to drive past the crowd at a snail's pace while accepting bouquets and allowing everyone to see her. In old age, public adulation is her

▼ *Queen Elizabeth II's 'annus horribilis' of 1992 included a hugely destructive fire at Windsor Castle.*

dynamo of life.

Her 90th birthday was a particularly jubilant occasion. A carnival parade with more than 200 floats representing all her life interests and charities threaded through London in front of large and appreciative crowds. Naturally, it included an Aberdeen-Angus bull.

Elizabeth made history, and gave hope to thousands of elderly people, when at the age of 92 she became one of the oldest patients ever to undergo a hip replacement operation. It was a complete success, as was the repeat performance when in 1998, even more remarkably, she had her other hip replaced at the age of 97 after a fall at Sandringham. Her grandson reported that, in the wake of both operations, which gave her a new and late lease on life, she had been able to resume Scottish country dancing at Balmoral. When Emperor Akihito of Japan visited London in 1998, the state banquet in his honour went on considerably longer than planned because, the Japanese ambassador reported, Elizabeth was so enjoying herself that she refused to go to bed.

Twice in 1995, crowds of at least 250,000 gathered in The Mall to commemorate the 50th anniversary of the end of the Second World War just as they had done in 1945. Thousands of proud, bemedalled veterans marched – including the Duke of Edinburgh, who felt it right to be among his old Far East comrades rather than take their salute. The deep drone of a Lancaster bomber filled the air.

The highlight of the celebrations was a moment of pure theatre. The first floor window of Buckingham Palace opened, and three women stepped on to the balcony. The Queen and Princess Margaret briefly held back, and the woman who had stood on that same balcony in 1945 with King George VI, her children and Churchill stood briefly alone in her moment of glory. As Dame Vera Lynn, in remarkably strong voice despite advancing years, sung *The White Cliffs of Dover*, accompanied by a quarter of a million voices stretching all the way up The Mall, Elizabeth mouthed the words with a tear glistening in her eye.

The crowd, of fighting veterans and of a generation not even born in 1945, cheered her to the echo; they were watching a living symbol of history, an archive photograph brought to life. It was as though some honoured but long-retired diva had made a guest appearance on the stage of La Scala. Most of the other players who epitomised the Second World War were gone; Elizabeth and Dame Vera Lynn were virtually the only two stars of that particular drama left alive.

Revitalised by two new hips and enjoying generally good health, Queen Elizabeth cruises effortlessly through her late nineties. She

Despite being within sight of her 10th decade, she revisited many of the places she had seen with her husband. She had been 17 at the time of the Bolshevik Revolution; she was still alive to witness the end of the Soviet Empire 72 years later.

▼ *With a young Prince Harry at Clarence House*

Elizabeth set a record for age on 14 June 1998, when she surpassed the late Princess Alice, Countess of Athlone, to become the longest-living member of the British Royal Family in history, at 97 years and 314 days.

maintains a gentle programme of engagements and frequent appearances at race meetings, but she was saddened by the deaths of close friends, particularly her bosom companion Ruth Fermoy and her faithful private secretary of more than 30 years, Sir Martin Gilliat. It is the inevitable consequence of great age.

Elizabeth set a record for age on 14 June 1998, when she surpassed the late Princess Alice, Countess of Athlone, to become the longest-living member of the British Royal Family in history, at 97 years and 314 days. Hairsplitters argued that the record did not count, since Elizabeth had been a royal only since her marriage in 1923, and there were no celebrations to mark the event. It is a noteworthy achievement nonetheless, and one that appears to confirm that an abundance of interests in life is an essential ingredient for prolonging it.

Born in the age of Victoria, Elizabeth has lived through six reigns, and is alive to see the future inheritor of the eighth reign, Prince William, grow into a young man of good looks and great dignity. By the time William ascends the throne, the office of constitutional head of state may be somewhat changed, its trappings reduced and the expectations of its public altered. But there is still likely to be some place for the virtue of public duty, dressed in the garb of sheer showmanship, that Elizabeth has displayed for almost an entire century.

▶▶ *The Queen Mother travels in her buggy between races at Sandown Park, 1998.*

FROM THE PAGES OF THE TIMES

HANDS ACROSS THE WALL SIGNAL AN END TO ISOLATION

NOVEMBER 14, 1989. At 8.20 on a cold, dank morning, the cruellest symbol of Europe's division and the long suffering of Berlin were swept away, with the first official handshake across a gap where once the Wall had stood, and a torrent of human freedom that streamed from East to West.

A vast crowd gathered to watch this latest breach in the Wall – the historic reopening of Potsdamerplatz, once the busiest crossroads in Europe. For 28 years it has been sealed shut by a deathly barren wasteland over which Western leaders gazed in silent horror from the finest viewing platform.

Herr Walter Momper, the Mayor of West Berlin, greeted his East Berlin opposite number, Herr Ebehardt Krack, as soldiers and border guard construction teams tore away the last slabs of this section of the concrete wall, levelled the ground and opened the old cobbled road, neglected and overgrown with weeds.

A vast crowd of East Berliners, who had waited behind a line of green-uniformed border guards, surged forward, barely pausing at the temporary checkpoint tent to have their passes stamped before running to the breach in the Wall,

almost blocked by cameramen, journalists and cheering West Berliners. Bells rang, Alpine horns sounded a triumphant welcome, the crowd sang and whistled and emotions flowed as freely as the champagne that greeted the astonished and delighted visitors. Young people sat astride the Wall, where until recently anyone approaching it would have been arrested, possibly even shot. Below, Berliners with hammers and chisels hacked away at the graffiti-covered concrete, chipping off souvenirs.

Gaping holes have already appeared through which the streams of people crowding up to the Wall gazed across at no man's land. The guards have almost disappeared and only army bulldozers, cranes and construction teams were to be seen yesterday. More than a million people were expected to stream through the Wall, now breached with nine new crossing points.

On Saturday some 800,000 East Germans crossed into the city, causing huge traffic jams and virtually bringing the city to a standstill as street parties thronged the famous Kurfurstendamm. Bands played, people embraced, and the big stores were overwhelmed with East Berliners gazing at unimaginable prosperity. West Berlin opened its hearts to its "fellow citizens from the East".

▶▶ *Queen Elizabeth II and Prince Philip enjoy the cheers of the crowd during their silver jubilee parade in June 1977. All over the country impromptu street parties were held to celebrate the event as Britain rediscovered its affection for the Royal Family.*

▪ *The warm response the Queen Mother receives from the crowds who turn out to wish her well on birthdays and to greet her at weddings has not diminished with* *the passing years. Her grandchildren and great-grandchildren are constant companions on these family occasions.*

▶ *The Queen Mother poses for photographers with her daughters and assorted grandchildren and great-grandchildren outside her official residence, Clarence House in London on her birthday, 4 August 1998. Front row, left to right: Princess Beatrice, Prince Harry, Queen Elizabeth II, the Queen Mother, Princess Eugenie, Princess Margaret and Lady Sarah Chatto. Back row, left to right: Prince Andrew, Prince Charles, Prince William, Prince Edward, Zara Phillips (just seen) and Daniel Chatto.*

Picture Credits

All the photographs reproduced in this book are held in the archives of *The Times* (TNL in the list below). The publishers wouyld like to thank the following organisations for their permission to reproduce those pictures held by *The Times* but not the property of *The Times*.Where there is no such acknowledgement, we have been unable to trace the source.

p. 10 St Paul's Walden Bury; p. 12 (top) TNL; p. 12 (bottom) Topham; p. 13 Central News; p. 14 Popperfoto; p. 15 Topham; p. 16 (top) Popperfoto; p. 16 (bottom left) Popperfoto; p. 16 (bottom right) Hulton Getty; p. 17 (top left) Topham; p. 17 (bottom left) TNL; p. 17 (right) St Paul's Walden Bury; p. 18 (top left) Popperfoto; p. 18 (top right and bottom) St Paul's Walden Bury; p. 22 Central News; p. 23 (right) Hulton Getty; p. 24 TNL; p. 26 (top and bottom) TNL; p. 27 TNL; p. 28 Photo Press; p. 29 TNL; p. 31 (top) St Paul's Walden Bury; p. 31 (bottom) Popperfoto; p. 32 (top and bottom) St Paul's Walden Bury; p. 34 (top) TNL; p. 35–37 TNL; p. 38 Topham; p. 40 (left) TNL; p. 41 (top) Judd; p. 41 (bottom) TNL; p. 43–46 (top left) TNL; p. 46 (top right and bottom left) Topham; p. 46 (bottom right) TNL; p. 47–54 TNL; p. 55 (top) Topham; p. 55 (bottom) – p. 58 TNL; p. 59 Popperfoto; p. 60–61 TNL; p. 62 (bottom) Press Association; p. 63–80 TNL; p. 81 Popperfoto; p. 82 –87 TNL; p. 88 (top) Topham; p. 88 (bottom) TNL; p. 89 Topham; p. 90–104 (top) TNL; p. 104 (bottom) Imperial War Museum; p. 105 (top) Topham; p. 105 (bottom) – 107 TNL; p. 108 Hulton Getty; p. 110–124 TNL; p. 126–127 TNL; p. 128 Hulton Getty; p. 130–135 (top) TNL; p. 135 (bottom) Planet News; p. 136–157 TNL; p. 158 Press Association.